Sew Pretty
Homestyle

D&C
David and Charles

A DAVID & CHARLES BOOK

Copyright © J.W. Cappelens Forlag, AS 2006
Cappelen Hobby
www.cappelen.no
Originally published in Norway as *Tildas Hus*

First published in the UK in 2007 by
David & Charles
David & Charles is an F+W Publications Inc.
company
4700 East Galbraith Road
Cincinnati, OH 45236

Reprinted 2007, 2008

A catalogue record for this book is available
from the British Library.

ISBN-13: 978-0-7153-2749-4 paperback
ISBN-10: 0-7153-2749-6 paperback

Printed in China by SNP Leefung
for David & Charles
Brunel House   Newton Abbot   Devon

Visit our website at www.davidandcharles.co.uk

David & Charles books are available from all
good bookshops; alternatively you can contact
our Orderline on 0870 9908222 or write to
us at FREEPOST EX2 110, D&C Direct, Newton
Abbot, TQ12 4ZZ (no stamp required UK only);
US customers call 800-289-0963 and
Canadian customers call 800-840-5220.

Welcome to My House

Of course, we're not afraid of going out in bad weather, but perhaps we just like to be in the comfort of our homes sometimes? You're welcome to join us. Instead of packing a lunch and going walking in the woods, jogging or cycling with the family, we prefer to enjoy ourselves in a different way – by sitting in a comfy chair with an inspiring book or a magazine to find ideas for yet another creative project.

As you know, you must never admit that a rainy day from time to time isn't a major crisis, because you mustn't joke about the weather – and sunny days are of course always welcome.

Even so, we are never bored, and new ideas and projects are an important source of joie de vivre and energy, which certainly has an effect on many areas of life and which will bring pleasure to those around us, either directly or indirectly.

With this book I hope to ensure that you won't run out of ideas in the near future, and I hope you'll enjoy the company of the book in your armchair on rainy days.

Here, you'll find a wide range of ideas for all the rooms in your house, as well as figures like sweet house angels, stumpy-legged dogs, cute cats, happy horses and good-natured teddy bears.

Notice that the various projects often pop up in new guises in different rooms from those where you find the instructions.

My dear dog, Matti, passed away just as I was beginning work on the book, and I really miss him; he was the inspiration for the dachshunds on page 28. After a while, though, there came the sound of new paws on the floor; this is Totto, who eventually allowed himself to be photographed on page 52.

Kind regards
Tone Finnanger

Contents

Fabrics and Materials

Fabrics

Fabrics with a slightly coarser weave are more suitable for stuffed figures than thinner materials, because they can be shaped more easily. For other projects, like mats, cushions, pouches, and suchlike, you can use all types of fabric. In this book, I have used mainly cotton fabrics and woollen felt, which can be bought in craft shops and can easily be combined with other fabrics, as shown here. Skin fabric is available in a light and dark version. Here I have used it to make angels, among other things.

Cotton padding – a soft, natural padding filler suitable for all quilted projects; it is also very useful for placing under material when you are embroidering or stitching.

High-volume vliselin – thin fibre felt with adhesive on one side which provides a stiff finish and is suitable for projects like wall pouches, which are not quilted but need a smooth, stiffened surface.

Vliselin – very thin, flat fibre felt with adhesive suitable for reinforcing thin materials or for making loosely woven fabrics sturdier and more stable. Vliselin has a stiffening effect on fabrics.

Thick fibre felt – 40mm (1½in) thick fibre felt is used for chair cushions and 20mm (¾in) thick felt for fabric boxes. Fibre felt can be flattened between two layers of material by pressing with an electric iron and helps to make fabric boxes stiff.

Vlisofix – the adhesive side is pressed against the reverse side of material with an iron and the paper is then torn off, resulting in an adhesive material for simple appliqué work. In this book, vlisofix is used for attaching patches and hearts on the dogs.

Cotton padding, high-volume vliselin, regular vliselin and vlisofix are obtainable from craft and sewing shops.

Embroidery yarn

In this book, embroidery and stitching are frequently used for decoration and a total of ten colours were used for these projects. Similar colours can be bought separately or in packs in embroidery and yarn shops, as well as in a number of sewing and craft shops.

Tape, buttons and drawstring holes

Mother-of-pearl buttons, mother-of-pearl press-studs, shaped buttons and drawstring holes have been used both for decorative and practical purposes. The most commonly used tapes in these projects are zigzag ribbon and synthetic leather thong.

Synthetic leather thong doesn't always stand heavy weights and in some cases should be replaced with a stronger material.

Tape, buttons and drawstring holes can be bought in craft outlets and sewing shops.

Face kits

Faces for figures found in this book can be easily made using face kits, which can be bought at many sewing and craft shops.

Disappearing ink pen

This pen is a valuable tool for tracing patterns onto fabric. The line disappears when you press it with a damp cloth, and also disappears of its own accord after a while.

Miscellaneous

Figure stands are used in this book for supporting figures, such as angels and horses, as well as for other characters in the book. The wooden rings used in the pin cushions can be bought in packs of large or small rings. Bag handles and stretcher frames can be bought in different shapes and sizes in craft shops.

Techniques

Embroidery and Stitching

For patterns for various embroidered items, see pages 126–127. For a pattern to fit a particular project, you should see the reference to the pattern page for that item.

If the material is thin, it may be necessary to iron a thin vliselin on the reverse side before embroidering a motif. This is not recommended on projects that are to be quilted. Use an embroidery ring for better control of the material wherever possible.

In roses and large 'propeller' flowers, fill in the surfaces with stitching, as evenly as possible. All the threads of the embroidery yarn should be used here, as in Figures A and B.

In small propeller flowers, a single stitch is enough to make each petal, as in Figure C.

French knots are used for the centres of the propeller flowers (using all threads of the yarn) and for dots in the stitched motifs (using a single thread).

Pass your needle and thread through the material and wind the thread between one and three times around the needle, depending upon how large you want to the French knot to be. See Figure D.

Stick the needle down through the material to about where the thread comes out and tighten the thread so that the turns are pulled right down to the material before you pull the needle through. See figures E and F.

Hair for appliquéd angels is embroidered using the whole yarn, as in Figure G.

Stems, lettering and stitched motifs, which are used, among other things, in the button bags on page 82, are sewn with small backstitches using a single thread. Cut a suitable length, grip one of the threads and pull it out. Sew a stitch on the top side and one backstitch, as in Figure H, then make two stitches forwards on the reverse side and one back on the top side, as in Figure I; then two stitches forward on the reverse, and so on.

Wrong Side Appliqués

The appliqués in this book are sewn on the wrong side, so that the frayed edge is not visible. This also makes the appliqués stronger while giving a fine three-dimensional effect. You can get almost the same effect by making a seam allowance around the parts that can then be folded inwards as you sew, but personally I think this is a more difficult process.

If you wish, a cheaper material can be used for the reverse side of the appliqués instead of the appliqué material, or liner material, as we call it here. This material should be relatively thin.

Place the appliqué material and lining together right side to right side. Trace the pattern for the appliqué item on the liner material and sew around it, as in Figure A. Cut out the figure and cut notches to where the seam curves inwards. Ideally, the seam allowance should be made as small as possible.

Cut an opening through the liner material for turning inside out, as in Figure B. If one side of an appliqué item is to be hidden under another item, leave this side open for turning inside out. See Figure C. For the long flower petals featured on the mat on pages 14–17, leave an opening at the bottom. In addition, you should cut a little way up on the wrong side to make it possible to turn it inside out, as in Figure D. Turn the parts completely inside out using, for example, a wooden stick. Place the parts on the backing and attach them with 'invisible stitches' as in Figure E. Finally, embroider and stitch the details as described above.

Quilting

All the quilting in this book has been done by hand using fairly large stitches. This provides a home-made effect and is actually quicker than you'd expect. When quilting, it's important to sew through all the layers so that the stitches are also visible on the reverse side.

Any appliqués and decorations must be finished before you do the quilting.

All stitches are short on the right side, about 1mm (1⁄16in), but vary in length on the wrong side, depending on the project in question. If you tighten the stitches as you sew, the material is gathered and produces a fine ruffled effect. This can be seen clearly in the table mat project on page 46. On projects where only parts of the surface are quilted, you should only tighten the stitches very slightly.

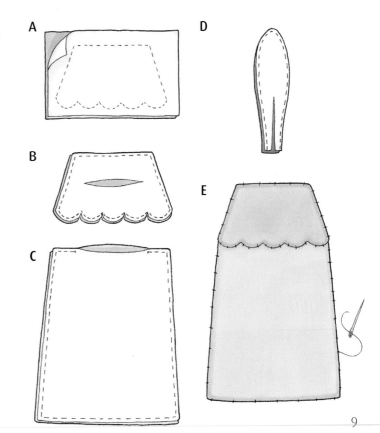

A

B

C

D

E

The longest stitches are 1.5–2cm (¾in) on the reverse side, and are used on the blanket and pillow project with the house motif and on the table mats. On tapestries and sleeping masks the stitches are shorter, 6–8mm (¼in) on the reverse side.

On the angels' wings, the stitches are 1–2mm (¹⁄₁₆in) long on the reverse side. This takes longer to do as the needle has to go all the way through the wing before you can push it upwards again; with longer stitches you can turn the point of the needle up and down sewing several stitches at once.

Transferring Patterns

There are many ways that you can transfer patterns, but for needlework projects, templates made of card or plastic are an obvious, simple solution.

Place a plastic sheet on the pattern and trace each of the various parts using a permanent marker, or place carbon paper between the pattern and a sheet of card, and transfer the pattern to the card. If you have access to a photocopier or scanner, the simplest solution is to make copies of the pattern pages and glue them on to card. If the pattern parts overlap, you will need to make several copies of each page. Take care to cut the templates accurately.

Transfer embroidery and stitching patterns by placing carbon paper between the pattern and the material, or hold the material up to the light so that you see the pattern through the material. A disappearing ink pen can also be used to draw patterns on material.

Scallop Borders

Many of these projects feature scallop borders. Here are some tips for making nice curves.

When making scallop borders, follow the instructions for the project. Be sure to use short stitches of around 1.5–2mm (¹⁄₁₆in) on the scallop borders. Cut off the seam allowance to leave only 3–4mm (⅛in) of seam allowance along the scallop border. Cut a notch between each curve as far in as possible without cutting through the sewing thread. Wiggle the scallops carefully back and forth so that the material wrinkles along the seam. Turn the scallop border completely inside out using a wooden stick inside the seam. Wiggle the scallops back and forth again after turning the border inside out so that any threads which may be under tension are loosened. Finally, iron the scallop border using a steam iron or place a damp cloth on it while ironing.

Stuffed Figures

The patterns in this book for dogs, cats, horses and angels all correspond to the smallest version. If you want to make larger versions, the patterns need to be enlarged using a photocopier or scanner. The larger versions are 120 per cent or 140 per cent of the original, and the size is always given in the instructions for the individual figure. Measurements in the instructions must be multiplied by the same percentage.

Avoid cutting out the figure beforehand unless completely necessary. Instead, fold the material over double and draw the figure on it using the pattern or template. Mark any openings for reversing or inserts if these are indicated in the seams on the pattern. If an internal opening is marked in the pattern, there should be no opening in the seam. Sew along the line in the drawing. Use a stitch length of 1.5–2mm (¹⁄₁₆in) and sew carefully, avoiding irregularities. See Figure A.

Cut out the figure; the seam allowance should be narrow, 3–4mm (⅛in) is best. However, where there are openings in the seam, a wider seam allowance, about 7–8mm (⁵⁄₁₆in), should be cut.

Where an internal reversing opening is marked in the pattern, it should be cut open as marked, through one of the layers of material.

Cut a notch in the seam allowance round the figure where the seam curves inwards, as in Figure B.

A wooden flower stick is useful as a tool for reversing and stuffing. The figures should be turned inside out by carefully pushing a flower stick along the seams after the figure has been reversed, so as to bring out all the details.

Fold in any extra seam allowance at openings and iron the parts before stuffing them.

Push stuffing loosely into the figure, avoiding pressing all the stuffing together into a lump before it is in position. The exceptions are small details like noses and thumbs, where it pays to form a small lump and push it into place before stuffing the rest of the figure.

A   B   C

Press the stuffing carefully but firmly into place and add more until you have a firm and well-shaped figure. Be aware that stuffing comes in a range of qualities and a good stuffing should not be too smooth or too sticky, but somewhere in between.

Finally, sew up the reversing openings, as in Figure C.

Faces

It is always best to wait until hair and ears have been attached before you make a face. This makes it easier for your to see where the eyes should be positioned. Stick two pins into the head to check where the eyes should

be. Remove the pins and fix the eyes in the pinholes. Use the eye tool from a face kit or the head of a pin dipped in black paint and punch on the eyes.

Rouge, lipstick or something similar can be applied with a dry brush to make rosy cheeks. Sew snouts on dogs, cats and teddy bears using pink embroidery yarn.

Fancy Hairdos

To make the fancy hairdos on angels you can use special dolls' hair available from crafts suppliers, along with thin steel wire.

The best way to start your angel's hairdo is to stick three long pieces of

steel wire through the doll's head so that you have six steel wires coming out. You can use a large bodkin to pull the wire through, as in Figure A. If this proves to be too difficult, just stick six lengths of steel wire well into the doll's head.

Tie a long piece of doll's hair around one of the six wires and twist the doll's hair back and forth on the back and top of the angel's head, eventually winding the hair around the wire ends too, as in Figure B. When you have covered the whole of the angel's head with doll's hair and wrapped hair some distance along each of the steel wires, bend the remaining uncovered wire in and twist it around itself close to the angel's head.

Finally, tack along the middle of the head with a few stitches to keep the hair in place. See Figure C.

You can give your angels hairdos with only two plaits by following the same procedure but by using just one or two lengths of steel wire instead of six as previously.

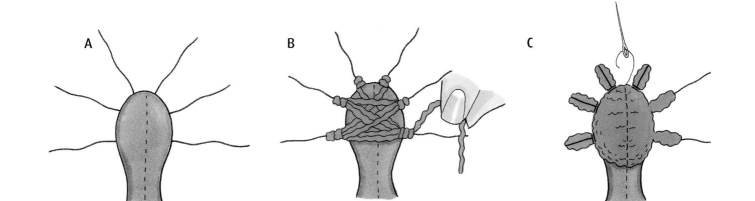

A   B   C

The Entrance Hall

The first room, and hence the first chapter in *Sew Pretty Homestyle*, is the entrance hall. Here you are met by some happy, if rather short-legged dogs.

You are welcome to borrow a pair of slippers, and put lavender-scented shoe hearts in your shoes while you are here, so that they smell good when you leave.

The floor mats are sewn from woollen felt and the bags are made in just the right sizes to contain the contents of handbags.

Welcome!

Floor Mats

The pattern is on page 127.

Pretty floor mats made from woollen felt are cosy and
decorative, but are not as solid as, for example, a rag rug,
and should therefore not be placed in the parts of the house
with most traffic.

NB: To avoid accidents in which you end up flat on the floor
or do the splits with the help of two adjacent mats, you
should apply some sort of anti-slip substance underneath.

You need:

Woollen felt
Cotton padding filler
Lining material
Materials for appliqués
Embroidery yarn for appliqués if desired
A bit of anti-slip material or relief liner

This is what you do:

The pattern on page 127 has been divided up so as to fit it
all on the page. Place the parts together so that the points
A and B lie adjacent to each other. The resulting pattern
element corresponds to one twelfth of the mat. Use a large
piece of card or similar, at least 67 x 67cm (26 x 26in), if
necessary taping several pieces together, and locate the
centre by measuring. Draw a cross, making sure that the
angles are exactly 90 degrees. Now draw three elements of
a pattern in each of the four fields between the arms of the
cross, as in Figure A, and cut out the template.

Cut a piece of woollen felt and a piece of cotton padding
large enough to cover the pattern, plus a seam allowance.
Cut two pieces of lining material half as wide as the pattern,
about 33.5 x 67cm (13 x 26in) and add a generous seam
allowance; sew the pieces of lining material together. Leave
a reversing opening at the centre of the seam, as in Figure
B. When the liner part is folded out, it should be the same
size as the felt and padding part.

Place the padding piece at the bottom, with the felt and
lining material on top, against the right side so that the
lining material is on top with the wrong side upwards. Fix
the parts together with pins, trace the pattern and sew
around the edge, as in Figure C.

Cut out and turn the mat inside out, as described under
'Scalloped Borders' on page 10.

Do not sew up the reversing opening until the appliqué
has been completed.

A

B

C

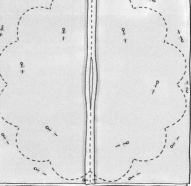

The appliqué on the mat is done in two ways; in one of the versions, there is a single flower in the centre, as in Figure D. The other version has several flowers with stalks sewn with embroidery yarn. See Figure E.

Appliqué the flowers as described on page 9. Draw the stalks freehand on the mat with a disappearing ink pen and sew with simple decorative stitches at the top and bottom. To prevent slipping you can draw with relief liner on the back of the mat or stitch on some anti-slip material, which is available in carpet shops.

D

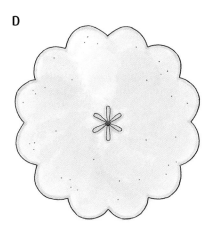

E

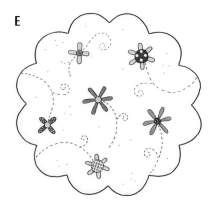

Slippers

The pattern is on page 128.

Sew these splendid slippers with woollen felt linings to offer to guests when they arrive at your home; this is particularly important when the floor has just been washed (for once?). The slippers have been tested on girlfriends of mine with shoe sizes ranging from 36 to 41, and they all say that they fit, though there may be some variation since feet come in all different shapes. My shoe size is 39 and the slippers fit me perfectly.

You need:

Material
Woollen felt
Thin vliselin for stiffening
Embroidery yarn for decoration if desired

This is what you do:

Iron the vliselin on the reverse side of a piece of material large enough for the soles, and cut them out according to the pattern. Remember that the soles of the slippers should be mirror images of each other, so that you have a left and right foot.Cut out the uppers of the slippers twice from the plain material. Now cut out two soles and two uppers from woollen felt using the dotted line. The felt lining will work best if it is slightly smaller than the outer material, since it takes up more space than the material.

Place the felt parts and material parts together right side to right side and sew along the curved opening. Cut notches along the curve so that it shapes better when it is reversed. See Figure A.

Fold the lining and material apart so the edges along the heel on each side can be placed against each other right side to right side. With lining against lining and material against material, sew the heel together as shown in Figure B. Turn inside out so that the right side is visible and sew a zigzag seam round the slipper parts to hold the lining and the outer material together. Make sure the edge of the felt lining is along the edge of the outer material all the way round; if necessary, pull it into position and fix it with pins before sewing. If you like, you can embroider decoration on the slippers as described on page 8. See Figure C.

Mark the middle of the upper part at the front and the sole part at the front and back as in the pattern. Place the upper part and the sole part right side to right side so that the seam on the upper part is adjacent to the mark on the back of the sole and the marks touch at the front. Fix the

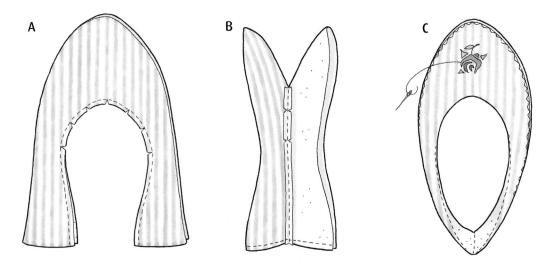

A   B   C

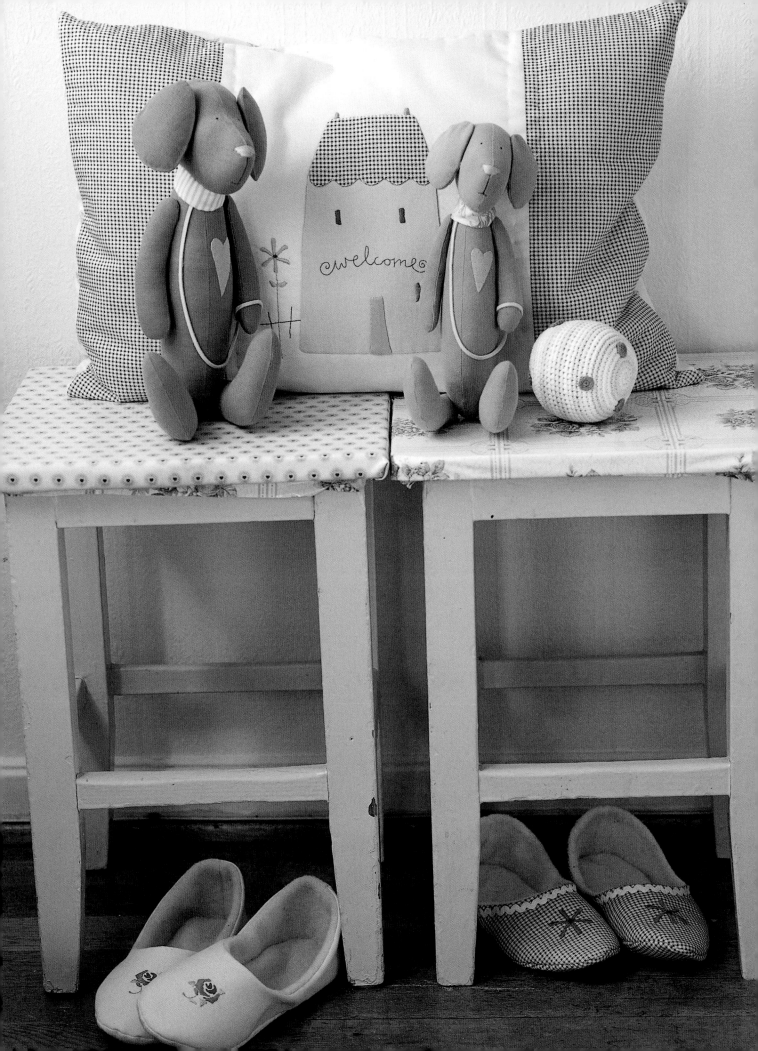

parts together around the edges with pins and sew the parts together as in Figure D.

Remove all the pins. Lay the woollen felt sole on top so that you have a sandwich of two soles with the slipper upper in the middle. Pull the felt sole so that the edges meet with those of the rest of the parts, fix with pins and sew round the edge. Leave an opening on one side for reversing, as in Figure E.

Cut away any surplus seam allowance round the edge and turn the finished slipper inside out.

D   **E**

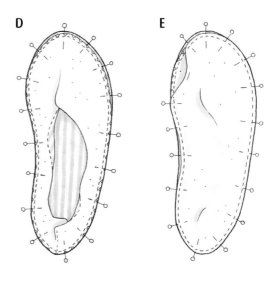

Hearts

The pattern is on page 128.

It seems impossible to me to make a book without hearts, but then they are the symbol of love. Hearts crop up throughout the book in various forms. Hearts for putting into shoes are described here, and embroidered hearts are sewn in the same way, but without loops. The attractive woollen felt hearts are sewn using the large heart pattern and are decorated with patches, buttons and short words from the 'My House' tapestry on page 54.

Hearts for shoes

I'm not trying to suggest that you have smelly feet, but I do think that sweet-smelling shoes are better than shoes with no smell at all. These shoe hearts are a excellent gift – as long as you explain this to the recipient.

You need:

Material
Thin vliselin
Stuffing
Dried lavender
Synthetic leather thong, or similar
Embroidery yarn for the stitched motif

This is what you do:

Cut two pieces of material big enough for the heart and iron vliselin on to the reverse side of each piece. Trace the stitched motif on one of the parts and stitch the motif as described on page 8.

Cut a strip of material about 3 x 7cm (1⅛in) x 2¾in), without seam allowance, and fold in the edges, as shown in Figure A. Now fold the strip double before sewing along one edge, to make a small loop, as in Figure B.

Place the two parts of the heart right side to right side and draw a little heart motif on the side where the stitching will be visible, so that the parts are correctly located relative to each other. Fold the loop double, place it between the layers as indicated on the pattern and sew round the heart. See Figure C. Remember to leave an opening to allow you to turn it inside out.

Cut out and turn the heart inside out as described on page 10. The other heart is sewn in the same way but without the stitched motif. Stuff with a mixture of lavender and fabric stuffing and sew up the opening. Tie the hearts to each end of a cord, about 50cm (20in) long.

A

B

C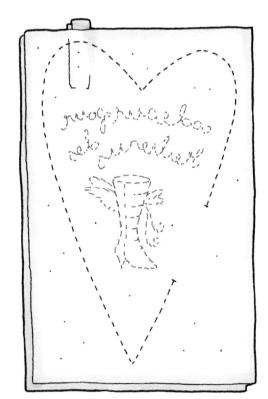

Bags

Personally, I cannot understand
how anybody can manage without small,
elegant bags near their entrance door; mine
quickly fill up with things that really don't have any other
logical place to be. I call them 'bag fillers'. I've never been
a particularly tidy person, and it's possible that I'm not
really normal as regards my bag fillers, but in my opinion
these bags are a perfect size. When the bag is full, you can
hang it as a decoration in the entrance hall and sew
yourself a new one ...

You need:

Material for the bag
Material for the lining
Round bag handles
Embroidery yarn or buttons for decoration if desired
(Needlework roses, see page 8)

This is what you do:

Cut two pieces of material and two pieces of lining material measuring 45 x 50cm (17½ x 20in) and add a seam allowance. If you want to use embroidery on the bag, you can do this on one of the material pieces as described on page 8. It is probably wise to reinforce the places where you intend to embroider using thin vliselin. Use an embroidery ring if you wish. Place the lining pieces right side to right side on the material pieces and sew them together along one 50cm (20in) edge. Sew 20cm (8in) down along each short edge, as in Figure A.

Fold the material and lining apart and place the two bag parts against each other so that material is against material and lining against lining. Use a plate of about 25cm (10in) diameter to draw rounded corners for the lining and material. Sew around the edges and leave a reversing opening in the lining, as in Figure B. Cut off the corners and surplus seam allowance and turn the bag inside out.

Draw a line 8cm (3in) from the edge of the fabric on the lining side using a disappearing ink pen. Fold the edge around the handle and tack it in place so that the edge coincides with the edge you have drawn, as in Figure C.

The roses on page 68 make a fine decoration for these bags.

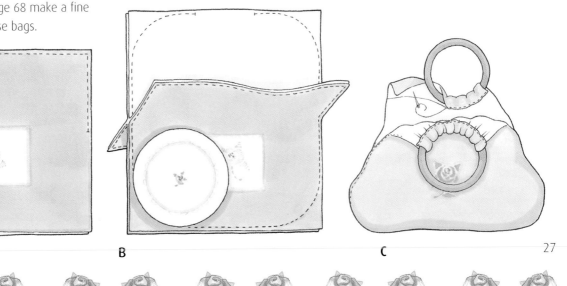

A   B   C   27

A

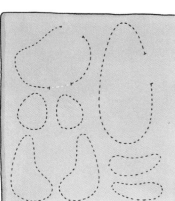

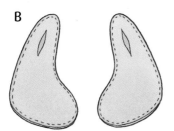

B

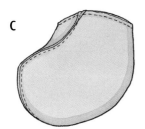

C

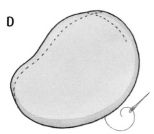

D

E

Dogs

The pattern is on page 129.

Dachshunds are marvellous animals. After having these dogs as pets for many years, all other breeds seem to have remarkably long legs! To me, their proportions are perfect.

You need:

Material for the body
Material for the dog-collar
Material for the heart
Vlisofix for the heart
Synthetic leather thong, or similar, for the leash
Stuffing
Embroidery yarn for the muzzle

This is what you do:

Read the section on stuffed figures on pages 10–11 and enlarge the pattern to 120 per cent if you want to make a large dog.

Fold a piece of material over so it is double thickness, trace the body, head, arms, legs and ears and sew around all the parts. Note that the V-shaped opening in the head should be open, as well as the reversing opening at the bottom of the head. See Figure A.

Cut out all the parts. Make a reversing opening through one layer of material for all the ears, legs and arms.

Cut the reversing openings on opposite sides so that you get a right and left version of paired parts. See Figure B. Turn inside out, iron and stuff all the parts except the head, and sew closed all the openings.

Fold the V-opening in the head the opposite way so that the seams lie above and below each other and sew it closed. See Figure C. Turn the head inside out, stuff it and sew up the opening, as in Figure D. Stuff the ears very loosely and iron them again so that they are almost flat.

Tack the head, arms and legs to the body so that the dog sits on its haunches and tack on the ears or attach them using a glue gun. Make the face as described on page 11.

Spread vlisofix on the reverse side of the material for the heart, draw the outline of the heart and cut it out. Attach the heart to the body using an iron and fix it with buttonhole stitching as in Figure E.

The dog's leash is a finishing touch. To make this, first cut a strip of material measuring about 10 x 4cm (4in x 1½in). Sew this in the same way as the loop for the heart on page 24 and tack it around the dog's neck. Cut a piece of cord and tie one end round one paw; then attach the other end under the collar.

The Kitchen

Ah ... I love being in the kitchen; it warms my heart to do domestic jobs like
baking, jam-making and so on with the radio on and flies buzzing around the window
frame. Or in the winter with the wood stove glowing and a cup of warm, sweet tea.
Here we have cats at play and pretty strawberries; lots of temptations ...

Cats

The pattern is on page 130.

I was a bit uncertain as to how much these resembled cats so I have embroidered the word 'cat' on their dresses. People have since confirmed that they do look like cats, so it's up to you to decide whether the word 'cat' is necessary.

You need:

Material for the body
Material for the dress and patch
Vlisofix for the patch
Stuffing
2 buttons
Embroidery yarn
Thin, black steel wire for whiskers

This is what you do:

For a large cat use 120 per cent of the pattern size. See Stuffed Figures on pages 10–11.

Sew the body, head, arms and legs in the same way as for the dog on page 28, but attach the legs firmly to the body with buttons and embroidery yarn, so that they are moveable. See Figure A.

Sew the tail and ears as in the pattern, fold in the seam allowance and push in a little stuffing material before tacking the ears to the head. See Figure B. Sew the tail on a little way up the rump, as in Figure C.

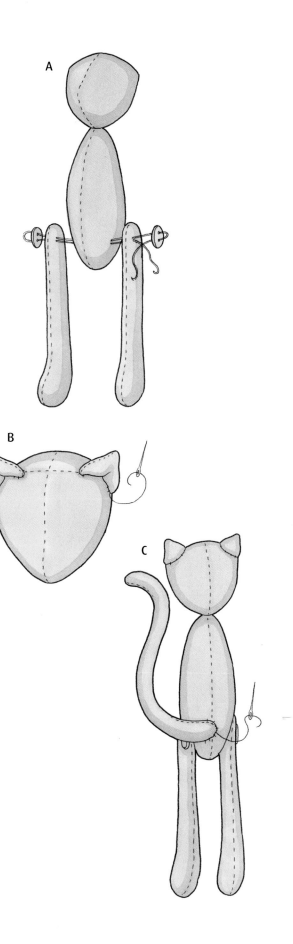

A

B

C

Cut a piece of material measuring 16 x 35cm (6¼ x 13¾in) for the dress, adding a generous seam allowance along the long edges. If desired, stitch the word 'cat' in the middle of the dress part and attach a patch with vlisofix and buttonhole stitching. Fold the dress double and sew it together. Leave a 4cm (1½in) opening in the seam, about 2.5cm (1in) from the bottom edge, as shown in Figure D, for attaching the tail. Sew around the tail opening, as shown in Figure E. Sew the seam allowance at the bottom of the dress and iron down the upper edge. Tack around the opening at the top and gather around the cat's neck. Sew the arms on to the outside of the dress. Make the face as described on page 11. Cut two pieces of steel wire for the whiskers and stick them through the muzzle so that they protrude on each side. Make curls in the wire and cut to length, as in Figure F.

D

E

F

Fragrant Strawberries

The pattern is on page 131.
(The pattern for the strawberry cushions for the children's room is on page 144.)

These fragrant strawberries are a nice gift idea. Drip a couple of drops of strawberry scent on each strawberry and put a few berries in a sealed jar. They can be taken out of the jar as needed to spread a pleasant aroma in the room. When the scent is used up, all you need to do is to add a couple more drops and they are as good as new.

You need:

Material for the strawberries
Material for the leaves
Stuffing
Embroidery yarn for the strawberry seeds
A few drops of strawberry scent, as desired

This is what you do:

Fold the material for the strawberry and for the leaves double and draw outline for the parts as in the pattern. Sew around the outlines, as shown in Figure A. Notice that the strawberry pattern is marked ES, meaning that extra seam allowance is to be sewn out on each side of the opening. Cut out the parts, make a reversing opening through one of the material layers on the leaf part and then turn the parts inside out.

Fold in the extra seam allowance around the opening on the strawberry and tack around the edge. Stuff the strawberry and gather the opening. Sew small seeds using red or white embroidery yarn.

Gather the leaf part using three stitches on the upper side, as shown in Figure B. Tack the leaves to the strawberry with the reversing opening downwards to conceal it, as shown in Figure C.

Strawberry scent for use in soap can be bought in craft shops and some pharmacies. If you like, you can drip a few drops on each strawberry.

A

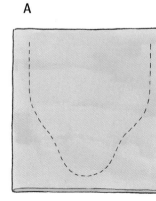

B

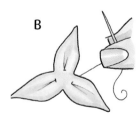

C

'Belles Tentations' Tapestry

The pattern for the motif is on page 131 and 132.

When it comes to beautiful temptations (such as Frenchmen and cakes), who can blame us for being a bit Francophile?

You need:

Materials for the backing and scallop borders
Material for the reverse side
Materials for appliqués
Cotton padding filler
Embroidery yarn for berries, leaves and lettering
Two rings for hanging, if desired

This is what you do:

The backing should measure 53 x 22cm (21 x 81½in); sew a strip, 22 x 5cm (8½ x 2in) long, to each end of the backing material. Add a seam allowance as shown in Figure A.

Cut a piece of material and a piece of cotton padding large enough to cover the whole backing and borders. Place the material and the backing material right side to right side with the padding underneath. Draw the scallop borders at each end as in the pattern and sew around the edges; see 'Scallop Borders' on page 10. Leave a large reversing opening on one long edge of the picture, as in Figure B. Cut away surplus seam allowance, turn inside out and iron the tapestry.

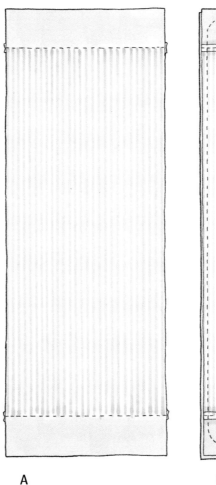

A   B

Begin by transferring and stitching 'La petite pâtisserie' (The little bakery) at the top, and then 'Belles tentations' (Beautiful temptations) at the bottom, as described on page 8. If you look at the pattern you'll see that I've drawn brackets to indicate where the words should be located relative to the backing material (ignoring the border).

Locate the centre of the tapestry and draw the ring at the top of the cake tray in relation to the upper text as shown in the pattern. Draw a line about 30cm (12in) long downwards from the ring and stitch everything using a full embroidery yarn, as in Figure C.

Sew the appliqués on the reverse side (three cake dishes with scallop borders in different sizes, three pink cakes and two cakes and cups) as described on page 9.

Place the two back-appliquéd sections in position and tack them to the backing. Embroider berries and leaves on the pink cakes. Sew up the reversing opening. Finally, quilt around all of the appliqués and around the edge of the picture as described on page 9.

Simple lifting curtains can be made from a piece of material with a wooden lath sewn at each end. Attach tapes at the top both in front of and behind the curtain and tie the curtain on each side. Attach screw eyes in the upper lath and screw hooks in the window frame for hanging.

C

The Dining Room

The dining room is the place for get-togethers with cakes, coffee and candlelight ... This room should have a certain style and for this you need a cover for the cafetière and hand-quilted table mats. There are also cushions so that the guests can sit comfortably while enjoying the fare.

Cafetière Cosy

Not so many years ago a whole range of new coffee variations entered our lives in the form of espresso, cappuccino, café latte, café mocha, and so on. Many of us bought a relatively cheap, but maybe slightly unreliable espresso maker, and hey presto – in a few minutes we could enjoy a café latte. After a while we found we couldn't be bothered to wait those few minutes every Sunday, and the novelty wore off. In my house we went as far as buying a cafetière, which is progress, after all.

You need:

Material for cafetière cosy and border
Tape
Cotton padding
Embroidery yarn for decoration

This is what you do:

Measure the circumference of the cafetière, making allowance for the handle, and then measure the height. See Figure A.

Cut two rectangular pieces of material and a piece of cotton padding with sides equal to the circumference times the height of the cafetière, adding a seam allowance.

Cut a strip of material for the scallop border, about 1cm (³⁄₈in) shorter than the circumference of the cafetière and 8cm (3⅛in) wide. Fold the strip double along its length and trace and sew the scallop border as shown on page 10. If desired you can transfer and embroider a motif as described on page 8. As you can see here I have placed the motifs in the centre of the right-hand half of the material. (See Figure C.)

Place the two pieces of material together, right side to right side, with the cotton padding underneath. Position the scallop border between the layers of material, along the upper edge. Draw a small curve in the centre of the upper edge, as in the pattern, and sew the materials together along the upper edge. The curve is there so that the cosy doesn't get in the way of the spout of the cafetière. Also sew together the bottom edges, leaving a reversing opening in the centre.

Cut six pieces of tape about 22cm (8½in) long and place three on each side, at the top, in the centre and at the bottom, before sewing the material layers together along the sides, as in Figure B.

Cut off the surplus seam allowance at the arc at the top, and around all edges. Remember to make some cuts towards the seam in the arc to avoid distortion caused by tension in the material.

Finally, turn the cafetière cosy inside out and sew the reversing opening closed, as in Figure C.

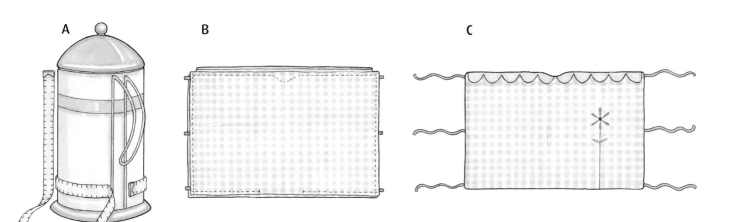

A

B

C

Table Mats

Table mats are a brilliant solution for those who aren't patient enough to iron tablecloths!

You need:

Material
Cotton padding filler
Embroidery yarn for roses

This is what you do:

Make the template in the same way as for the floor mats on page 14.

Cut some material, large enough to cover the template twice, adding seam allowances. Fold the material double, right side to right side, and sew it together along the open edge, leaving a reversing opening in the seam, as shown in Figure A.

Fold the material so that the seam is in the centre and iron the seam allowances to either side. Place a piece of padding material large enough to cover the template under the material. Trace the pattern and sew around the edge, as in Figure B. Cut out and turn the table mat inside out, as described under 'Scallop Borders' on page 10. If desired, embroider a rose as described on page 8 and sew up the reversing opening.

Quilt the table mat first along the scallop border and then in circles towards the centre as described on page 9. To produce a ruffled effect, tighten the thread as you quilt. See Figure C.

A

B

C

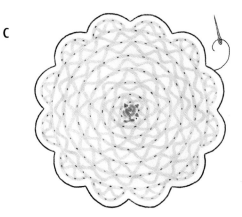

Chair Cushions

Comfy chair cushions in classic style, suitable for commoners and kings, kitchens and dining rooms. Princesses prefer round cushions with embroidered roses; remember to place a pea under the cushion, as in the fairy tale, to check for frauds.

You need:

Material
About 40cm (15½in) of thick fibre felt
Embroidery yarn

This is what you do:

The cushions should be cut to a size of about 35 x 35cm (13¾ x 13¾in); after sewing and quilting the size will be about 33 x 33cm (13 x 13in). Cut a piece of material twice as large as the template, adding seam allowances.
Fold the material double and sew it together along the open edge, leaving a reversing opening in the seam.
Fold the material so that the seam is in the centre and iron the seam allowances to either side. Place the material on the padding, with the opening at the top.

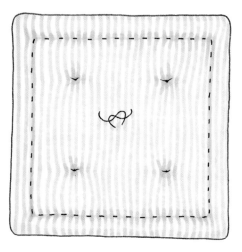

Sew around the edges of the cushion. Cut off the surplus seam allowance and then turn the cushion inside out through the opening.

Quilt around the cushion using embroidery yarn, about 3.5cm (1½in) from the edge. Stitch through the cushion and tie knots about 14cm (5½in) in from each corner, and a knot in the centre, as shown in the illustration (left). Cushions of all sizes can be made in this way. To make round cushions, use an object about 34cm (13½in) in diameter to trace a circle on the material, quilt 3.5cm (1½in) in from the edge and tie a knot in the centre.

Pictures and Boards

Pretty pictures and beautiful boards are easy to make with a frame covered with fabric. Empty frames are available in various sizes from most craft stores.

Start by embroidering your choice of image on a piece of fabric. Make sure your fabric is large enought to pull over the frame and attach to the back. Pull the fabric tightly over the frame and to the back. Attach with a staple gun. Cut off any excess material.

If you are making a message board, decorate it with ribbons in a criss-cross pattern attaching any loose ends on the back. Secure the ribbons through the board where they cross over, using buttons or pearls.

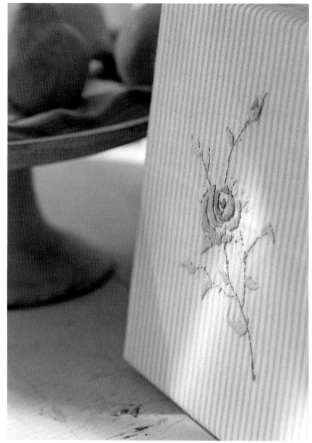

The Living Room

Sit yourselves down and take out your needlework – the coffee's nearly ready; and yes, you are allowed to put your feet up on the table!

In the living room you'll find the largest project in this book: the 'My House' tapestry is embroidered, stitched and hand-quilted, and is a piece of work you can easily do while sitting comfortably on your sofa.

There's also the occasional house angel to be found here.

'My House' Tapestry

This tapestry has become one of my favourites, but it has to be said that it is the biggest project in my books so far. If you are going to enjoy making it, you need to be aware that it takes some time, as it involves embroidery, stitching and hand-quilting. For enthusiasts, all this is pleasurable work to do while sitting on a sofa.

Those of you who are good at using a sewing machine will be able to reduce the working time by doing the wording and quilting on your machines, but I don't think this brings the same satisfaction.

The tapestry motifs are also very suitable for cushions.

You need:

Nine different types of material for backing
Material for the reverse side
Material for the border
Cotton padding for stuffing
Various materials for appliqués
Various embroidery yarns

This is what you do:

Backing pieces

The finished tapestry measures 120 x 180cm (47 x 71in) and is made up from nine different rectangles creating two rows. The rows are repeated, one of them three times and the other rows twice, making a total of five rows in all. The rectangles in each row are located in reverse order when the row is repeated, so as to create a good balance in the tapestry. The different numbered motifs can be seen in Figure A. Use the dimensions shown below, adding seam allowances:

Rectangle 1, 15 x 32cm (5½ x 12½in) x 4
Rectangle 2, 30 x 32cm (12 x 12½in) x 3
Rectangle 3, 15 x 32cm (5½ x 12½in) x 2
Rectangle 4, 40 x 32cm (15½ x 12½in) x 3
Rectangle 5, 25 x 32cm (10 x 12½in) x 2
Rectangle 6, 15 x 32cm (5½ x 12½in) x 2
Rectangle 7, 30 x 32cm (12 x 12½in) x 2
Rectangle 8, 30 x 16cm (12 x 16¼in) x 2
Rectangle 9, 30 x 16cm (12 x 16¼in) x 2

A

B

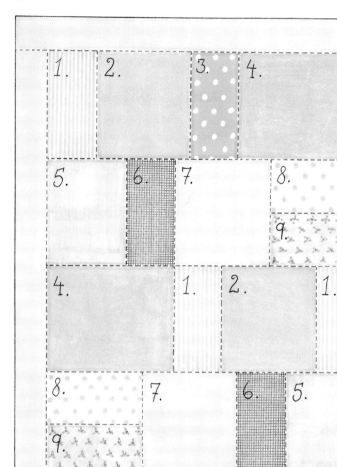

Figure B shows how the different numbered rectangles should be sewn together. Start by cutting the different sized rectangles to the dimensions shown on page 55 and sewing the parts of the backing together. Then sew a 10cm (4in) border around the backing material, allowing a generous seam allowance.

Motif

The house pattern on page 133 is cut in the middle by a fold line to fit to the page, and the parts should be twice as big as shown.

Sew the wrong side appliqués as described on page 9. Place the appliqués about 5.5cm (2¼in) from the lower edge of each rectangle and sew them in place.

The doors are too narrow to be sewn inside out, instead you should cut them with a seam allowance, which is folded inwards as you sew them in place on the houses.

Find the various embroidered and stitched details in the pattern. These should be located as shown in Figure A (previous page). See also the photographs of the tapestry. Work on one rectangle at a time. Transfer the motif, stitch and embroider the details as described on page 8.

C   **D**   **E**   **F**

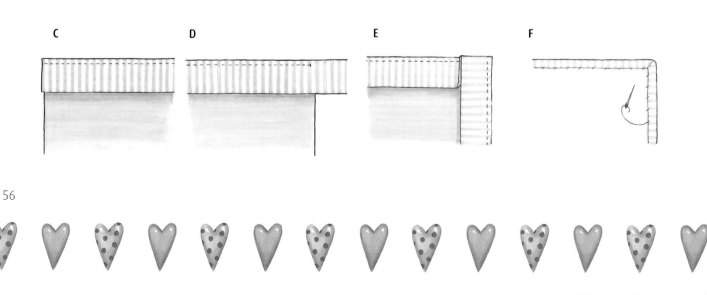

Padding and backing piece

Spread out a piece of material large enough for the whole tapestry with the right side down. On top of this place an equally large piece of cotton padding material and finally the completed appliqué tapestry on top with the right side up and the wrong side against the padding. Make sure that all the edges are aligned and iron the tapestry so that it is completely smooth. This is best done on the floor.

Using a large needle and large stitches, sew horizontally and vertically across the tapestry at 20–25cm (8–10in) intervals, so that the tapestry, padding and backing material are fastened together. This groundwork is important if everything is to stay in place while you are quilting the tapestry.

The tapestry is hand-quilted using relatively large quilt stitches (see page 9). First, quilt along the seams and then about 1.5cm (½in) in from each side of each seam.

Border

When you have completed quilting the tapestry, cut off the surplus seam allowance around the edge, leaving a border of exactly 10cm (4in) all round the tapestry. Sew a wide zigzag seam around the edge to keep the layers neatly together.

Cut 4cm (1½in) strips of material and sew them together until you have enough to go around the whole tapestry, about 6 metres (6½ yards) altogether. Start in one corner, placing the material strip right side to right side against the motif side of the tapestry. Sew on the strip about 6cm (2½in) from the edge, as shown in Figure C.

When you get to a corner, stop your seam about 6cm (2½in) from the edge, as shown in Figure D. Fold the strip, as shown in Figure E, before continuing sewing. When the strip has been sewn in place round the entire tapestry, fold it in round the edge and tack it to the back, as in Figure F.

Angels

The pattern is on pages 134–135.

I dream about small, helpful house angels who flit around with one purpose in mind – to make life simpler for the residents of the house. Some days you can almost sense that they're there, while on other days …

You need:

Material for the body
Materials for the clothes and slippers
Woollen felt for sweater
Hair and steel wire
Stuffing

This is what you do:

Most of the angels in this book are sewn in the original size, except the one in the kitchen on page 41, for which the pattern has been enlarged to 140 per cent.

Body

Read the general instructions for stuffed figures on page 10. Fold the skin fabric double and trace the body, arms and legs from the pattern in the same way as for the dog on page 28; sew around the parts. Cut out the parts, turn them inside out and iron them. Stuff the legs up to the dotted line on the pattern and sew a seam straight across before stuffing the rest of the leg, as in Figure A. Stuff the body, fold in the seam allowance around the opening and insert the legs. Only the lower part of the arms should be stuffed, so that the arms hang nicely when the angel has been dressed up, and so that they can be bent and fixed at the desired angles. Tack on the legs and arms, as in Figure B.

Pantaloons

Cut out the parts of the pantaloons as in the pattern, adding a seam allowance at the waist and at the bottom of the legs. Note that the parts should be double, so that the fold is in the centre of each of the two pieces. Place the two parts right side to right side and sew them together as shown in Figure C. Fold the pantaloons so that the seams are on top of each other and sew the legs as shown in Figure D.

Fold open the seam allowance at the bottom of the pants, remove small pieces of glue from the backing paper of vlisofix (see page 6) and push them into the fold on either side. Iron the fold so that it sticks.

Turn the pantaloons inside out, put them on the figure and tack them round the waist.

A   B

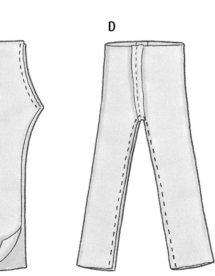

C   D

Skirt

Cut some material measuring about 40 x 25cm (15½ x 10in), fold it double, right side to right side, and sew the edges together on the open side. Sew the seam allowance around the edge. Put the skirt on the angel, fold pleats at the waist and fix with pins before tacking the skirt in place.

Sweater

Note that the pattern for the sweater is marked with a fold line and should be cut double. Woollen felt doesn't fray, so seam allowances at openings aren't necessary at the places marked with dotted lines on the pattern.

Place two pieces of felt, large enough for the sweater, right side to right side and trace the pattern. Sew around the outline of the sweater as shown in Figure E. Cut out the sweater and turn it inside out. Put the sweater on the angel, as shown in Figure F, then fold the collar of the sweater double inwards towards the angel's neck, as in Figure G. Then fold half the double collar out again, as in Figure H.

E

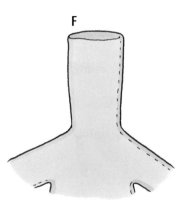

F

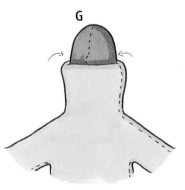

G

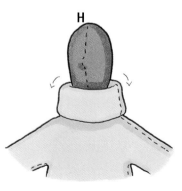

H

Slippers

Fold material for the slippers right side to right side. Trace the shape, sew and cut the curve at the opening of the slipper as shown in Figure I, then turn the slipper so that the right side is out. Fold the part double so that the fold is in the middle, as shown with a dotted line on the pattern. Trace half the slipper and sew round it as shown in Figure J, then cut out the slipper and press the toe flat using an iron. Trace the small curve in the pattern so that the toe of the slipper is rounded and sew it as shown in Figure F, before cutting the toe on the outside of the seam. Turn the slipper inside out so that the seam is inside. If desired, embroider a small flower on the slipper, like those of the 'Dressing Gown Angels' on page 103. See Figure L.

Wings

Cut out a piece of material twice as large as the wings and a piece of cotton padding the size of the wings. Fold the material double right side to right side and place the cotton padding underneath. Trace the pattern on the material and sew around the edge, as in Figure M. Cut out the wings and turn them inside out before sewing up the reversing opening. If you wish, quilt small flourishes as shown in the pattern; see page 9.

Tack or glue the wings to the angel and attach the slippers with a couple of stitches at the back.

You can make a fancy hairdo and a face for your angel as described on page 11.

I

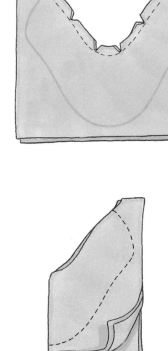

J

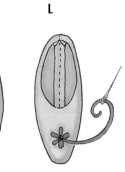

K   L

M

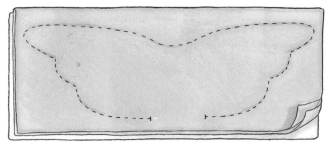

62

The Conservatory

Everybody should have a conservatory with beautiful flowers that bloom all the year round.

If you don't have a suitable room, you can make a little garden layout on a table near a patio door or window.

In my conservatory you'll find pears from the garden, roses and a garden angel who flits around looking after everything that grows. The horses were also given space here, because they wanted to be close to the garden outside.

Pears

The pattern is on page 136.

Needlework pears make nice decorations in a bowl or arranged on a cake tray. You can also decorate them with patches or the words 'une poire'.

You need:
Material for the pear
Material for the leaf
Stuffing
Flower stick
Embroidery yarn
If desired, material and vlisofix for a patch or embroidery yarn for decoration

This is what you do:
Fold the material for the pear and the material for the leaf double and draw the parts as in the pattern. Sew around the outline as shown in Figure A. Notice that the pear pattern is marked ES, meaning that extra seam allowance is to be sewn out on each side of the opening. Cut out the parts and turn them inside out.

Fold in the extra seam allowance around the opening on the pear and tack around the edge. Stuff the pear and gather the opening. Use a long needle, pull embroidery yarn from underneath right through the pear. Push the yarn back again and tie the two ends of the yarn together under the pear, tightening them to form a small hollow on the top of the pear. See Figure B.

Cut about a 5cm (2in) piece of flower stick and sharpen one end. Twist the pointed end down into the hollow on the top of the pear so that it penetrates the material and stays in the pear. Tack on the leaf as in Figure C and decorate the pear with a patch, words, or similar.

A

B

C

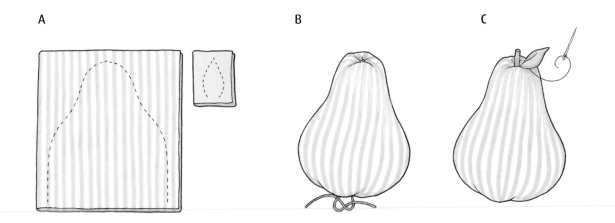

Roses

The pattern is on page 136.

Needlework flowers never fade, are perfect gifts and can, like strawberries, be drizzled with rose scent to freshen the air in the room. They also make pretty decorations for hats, handbags and scarves.

You need:

Material for the rose
Material for the leaf part
Embroidery yarn

This is what you do:

The large rose pattern has been divided in two to fit on the page. Place the two parts together so that the points A and B lie adjacent to each other. Both the large and the small rose pattern are marked with a fold line and should be doubled over. The pattern for the large rose is about a metre (39¼in) long altogether and the small one is about 58cm (22¾in).

Cut a strip of material twice the width of the rose pattern and fold it double. Trace the rose pattern and sew around the outline, leaving a reversing opening in the straight seam, as in Figure A.

Cut out the rose, turn it inside out and iron it. Begin by rolling a couple of times at one end and secure with embroidery yarn before continuing to tack along the edge, as in Figure B.

Gather the material before rolling up and make sure you secure it as you go gather it it up. See Figure C. When the whole rose has been gathered and rolled up, sew all the layers of material together securely by using stitches back and forth under the rose. Fold the outer turns of fabric down so that the rose becomes wider and more of the inner layers of the rose become visible, as shown in the photograph above.

Fold the material for the leaf part double, trace the pattern carefully on to the material and sew around the outline. Cut out the leaf part for the rose, make a reversing opening through one of the material layers and then turn the leaf part inside out. Tack the leaf part under the completed rose.

A

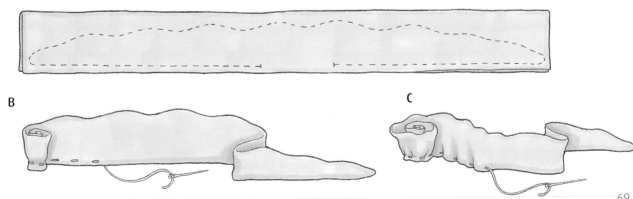

B

C

Horses

The pattern is on page 137.

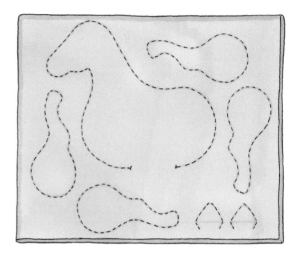

A

These horses gallop, free and contented, through the conservatory.

You need:
Material for the body
Material for patches
Stuffing
Rope or similar for hair
Paint in a slightly darker shade than the material
for the body
Embroidery yarn for wording
Figure stand

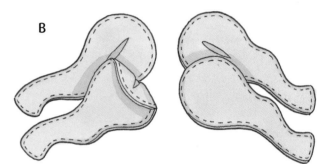

B

This is what you do:
The large horse is 120 per cent of the original size.
To make it easier to get a smooth finish, use thin vliselin to reinforce the material before sewing the horse together.

Fold the material for the horse double, right side to right side, and trace the body, ears and four legs. Sew around the parts, as shown in Figure A, and cut them out. Make a reversing opening through one of the material layers on each leg, remembering to do it on the other side of two of the legs, to make left and right legs. See Figure B. Turn inside out, iron and stuff the parts, then tack the openings closed.

Mix a paint that is slightly darker than the material for the body, for example, use brown and white for a light horse, and brown and black for a dark horse. Paint the horse's muzzle and hooves.

Attach patches to the horse using vlisofix and a hot iron and sew buttonhole stitching around the edges of the patches. If desired, transfer and stitch the words 'My horse' as described on page 10. Tack on the legs.

Fold in the seam allowance at the base of the ears, stuff them with padding and fold the ears double. Tack the ears on to the head. Make a bundle of string and tack it on between the ears before cutting it to shape with scissors, as in Figure C.

C

Sew on a bundle of string to form a tail and cut to a suitable length. Sew a cross of dark brown thread on the muzzle to form nostrils and make a face as described on page 11. Sharpen the stick of the wooden figure stand with a pencil sharpener and then push and twist some distance into the horse.

Garden Angels

The pattern for the jacket is on page 134.

A day-dreaming garden angel goes well in the conservatory, a room that for most of us is more for pleasure than utility.

The instructions below are for making the details that differ from those of the angel on pages 58–63, that is, the jacket, scarf and apron. Instructions for the roses are on page 68. Sew the body, pantaloons, skirt, slippers and wings as for the angel on pages 58–62.

Apron

You need:

Material for patches and apron
Vlisofix for the patches

The apron measures 20 x 14cm (8 x 5½in), plus a seam allowance. Fold and sew the edges of the apron; if desired attach a patch to the apron using vlisofix and sew round it with buttonhole stitching or similar. Attach the apron with some pleats at the waist in the same way as for the skirt.

A

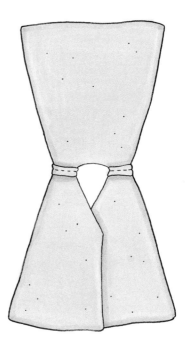

B

C

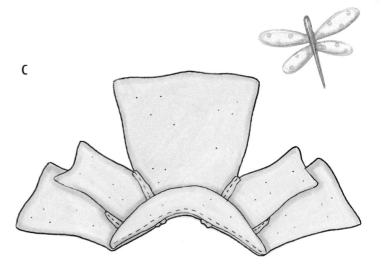

D

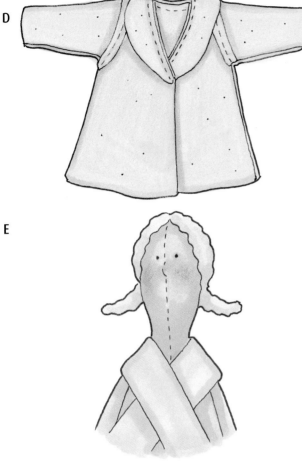

E

Jacket and scarf

You need:

Woollen felt for the jacket
Cord (synthetic leather thong or similar) for the jacket
Material for the scarf

N.B. The same pattern is used for the dressing gown on pages 102–103. A dotted line marks the end of the jacket.

Cut out two front pieces, one back piece, two sleeves and a collar. Woollen felt doesn't fray, so only give a seam allowance where parts will be sewn together. Edges where there is no seam allowance have dotted lines on the pattern.

Sew the front pieces to the back piece as shown in Figure A and then sew on the sleeves as in Figure B.

Stretch out the collar and place the right side against the wrong side of the jacket and sew together at the neck, Figure C. Fold the jacket double, right side to right side, and sew together on each side, Figure D. Then turn inside out.

For the angel's scarf cut a piece of material, fold it double and attach it around the neck before the jacket is put on, as in Figure E. Put the jacket on the angel and tie a tape around the waist to keep it in place.

Coat hangers made from fairly soft wood are available from craft shops and can be used to make attractive rows of coat hooks, see the photo below.

Use wooden laths and nails to make garden signs. A rustic appearance can be obtained by rubbing brown colour into the wood before painting it in a lighter colour using an almost dry brush.

The Hobby Room

The hobby room is probably the heart of my house. Here you can find smart and useful items that also make fine gifts for girlfriends – pin cushions, needle cases and button bags, among other things.

The decorative wall pouch board is made using a stretcher frame.

Pin Cushions on Wooden Rings

These pin cushions are inspired by similar items from the 1950s and stand firmly on a wooden ring base. On the pattern pages you can find a stitching motif in a suitable style and shape.

If you have a good, soft armchair that you enjoy sitting and sewing in, you can attach the pin cushion to the arm with pins, so it is ready whenever you need it.

You need:
Wooden ring (available from craft suppliers)
Material for the ring
Material for the pin cushion
Embroidery yarn
Stuffing

This is what you do:
Cut a strip of material wide enough to cover the edge of the ring and long enough to go round its circumference. The material will ruffle a little around the ring when it is sewn on, so make the strip of material a little longer than the circumference. Add a seam allowance to the width, so that one edge of the material can be folded in and tacked over the other, as in Figure A.

Trace a circle on the material for the pin cushion, two and a half times as wide as the wooden ring, so if the ring is 10cm (4in) in diameter, the circle of material should be 25cm (10in). Add a seam allowance and cut out. Embroider or stitch the motif in the centre of the circle of material as described on page 8.

Tack around the circle using embroidery yarn, gather it loosely and stuff the cushion. Now gather it more tightly together and stuff in more padding until the cushion is firm. Tack back and forth on the bottom of the cushion until it is as round as possible.

Press the ring against the underside of the cushion and fix it in place by tacking the material covering the ring to the cushion itself. Avoid sewing around the ring, but instead sew between the cushion and the ring, as in Figure B.

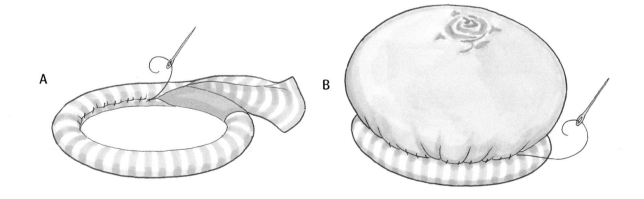

A

B

Needle Case

The pattern is on page 138.

These attractive needle cases hold your needles safely in several layers. The case itself is reinforced with stiffening vliselin to prevent the needles from penetrating though the material. Press-studs make opening and closing the case easy when in constant use.

You need:

Material for the outer cover
Material for lining and middle layer
Thin vliselin for stiffening
Press-studs
Embroidery yarn or similar for decoration

This is what you do:

Cut a piece of material for the outer cover of the needle case and a piece of lining material large enough to cover the pattern. Iron thin, stiffening vliselin on to the wrong side of the material. Place the material with attached vliselin and the lining material right side to right side, trace the pattern and sew around the outline, leaving a reversing opening. See Figure A.

Fold a piece of the same material as used for the lining right side to right side; trace two middle pieces and sew around the outlines. Cut out the pieces and turn them inside out before sewing up the reversing openings. Locate the centre of the middle pieces and sew them into the needle case, as marked with a dotted line on the pattern. See Figure B.

Fold the lower part of the middle pieces double and turn the wings on the needle case in towards the centre. Now fold the lower part of the needle case up and the lower part down over it. Press the folded case with an iron to form creases.

If desired, embroider a small motif on the needle case as described on page 8, remembering to allow space for the press-studs. Mark the position of the press-studs as in the pattern, checking that the position of the two parts agrees, and attach them according to the instructions that come with them.

A

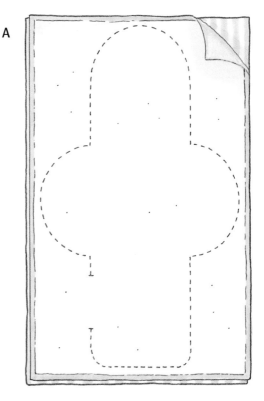

B

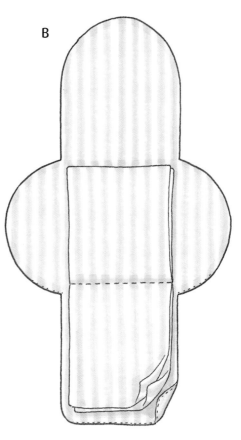

Small Button Bags

Small needlework bags are of course useful for more than just buttons. These bags can be made very quickly with no motif. Remember that they can also be made in other sizes, to form shoe bags, pyjama holders, spectacle cases, and so on. This size is also perfect as a lavender or soap bag.

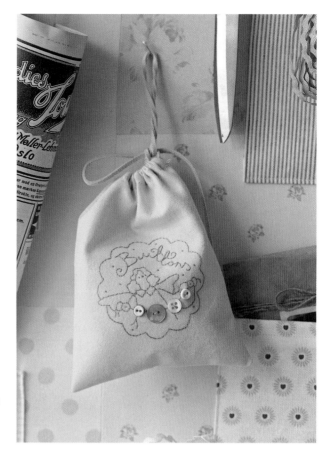

You need:

Material for the bag
Cord
Embroidery yarn and buttons for the motif
Thin vliselin if required

This is what you do:

Cut out a piece of material measuring 24 x 17cm (9½ x 6¾in) and add a seam allowance. The material will be folded double, the finished bag being 12cm (4¾in) wide. So locate the motif in the centre of the right-hand half, about 3cm (1in) from the bottom. When positioning the motif, it is important to remember that the seam allowance will not be there on the finished bag. Stitch the motif as described on page 8. If necessary, use vliselin to reinforce the material where the motif is to be stitched.

Measure 3cm (1in) from the top edge of each side, cut a notch in the seam allowance, fold the seam allowance in towards the reverse side of the material and sew it in place, as in Figure A.

Fold the edge inwards and down, insert the cord and sew the edge to the reverse side, as in Figure B. Fold the bag double, right side to right side, and sew it together. See Figure C. Turn the bag inside out and iron it. For a further touch, you can sew an assortment of real buttons over some of the stitched buttons.

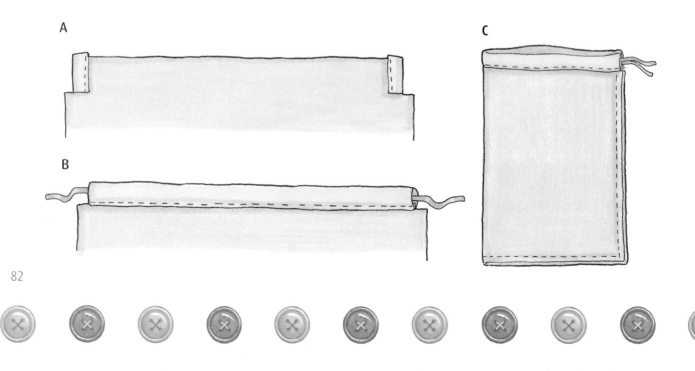

Fabric Boxes

A

You need:

Material

About 20mm (¾in) thick fibre felt

Cardboard for the base, cut from a cardboard box, for example

This is what you do:

Small box: material 64 x 48cm (25½ x 19in); fibre felt 64 x 24cm (25½ x 9½in); cardboard 18 x 4cm (7 x 1½in). Large box: material 100 x 75cm (39¼ x 29½in); fibre felt 100 x 37cm (39¼ x 14½in); cardboard 28 x 21cm (11 x 8¼in).

Make plenty of seam allowance on all edges of the material pieces, but only on the short edge of the fibre felt.

B

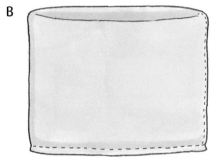

Place the strip of fibre felt so that it covers half of the wrong side of the piece of material. Fold everything double, right side to right side, and sew up the open side as in Figure A. Fold the material part down over the material/felt part all the way round and press with an iron to make the fibre felt flatter and more compact between the layers of material. Sew all the layers together at the bottom. See Figure B.

Fold the material to make a corner on each side for the base and sew across the corner 7cm (2¾in) in from the tip for the small box and 11cm (4¼in) in for the large one. See Figure C. Cut off the corners on the outside of the seam and turn the box inside out so that the seams in the base and corners are inside the box. Cover the cardboard base with material and tack it on the back. Push the card base down to the bottom of the bag, hiding the seams on the bottom. Finally, fold the edge down around the box for extra reinforcement, about 4cm (1½in) for the small box and 5.5cm (2¼in) for the large one. Press with an iron.

C

Fabric Tags

The pattern is on page 138.

You need:
Material
Cotton padding
Drawstring holes, about 6mm
(¼in) diameter
Cord

This is what you do:
Fold a piece of material large enough to cover the pattern double, right side to right side, and place it on top of a piece of padding large enough to cover the pattern once. Trace the pattern and sew around the edge, leaving a reversing opening. Cut out, turn inside out and iron. Attach a drawstring hole as described on the packaging.

The Bathroom

The morning sunshine peeps in through the bathroom window. Here you'll find instructions for a pompadour, which holds toiletries in tall containers, an attractive wall tapestry advertising 'Angel Rose Water', a make-up bag and small wall pouches, as well as a couple of sleepy dressing gown angels waiting for their turn.

Some people might enjoy being up bright and early, but perhaps not these angels!

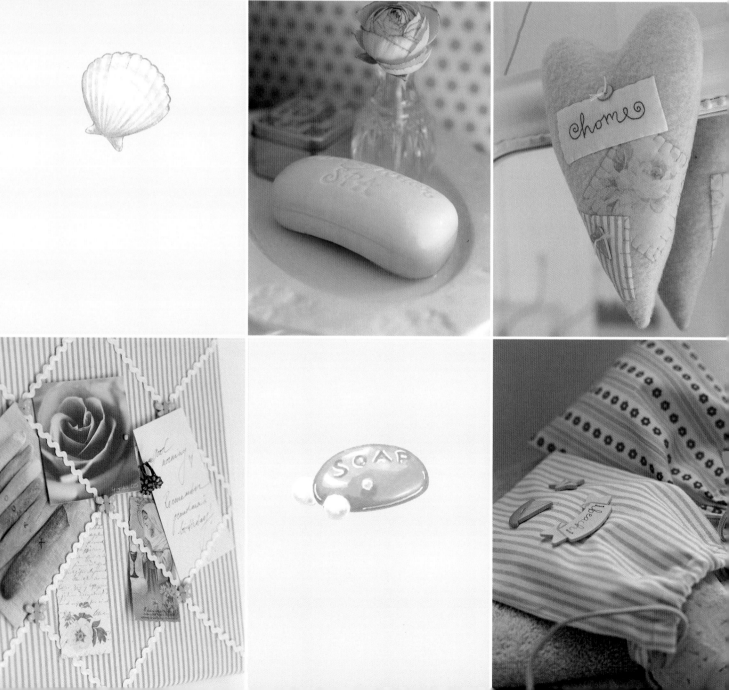

Pompadour

The pattern for the angel appliqué is on page 139.

You need:

Material
Lining material
Material for the drawstring edge
Cotton padding
Embroidery yarn
Material for decoration if desired
Cord
Drawstring holes – two of 6mm (¼in) and one of about 11mm (½in) diameter

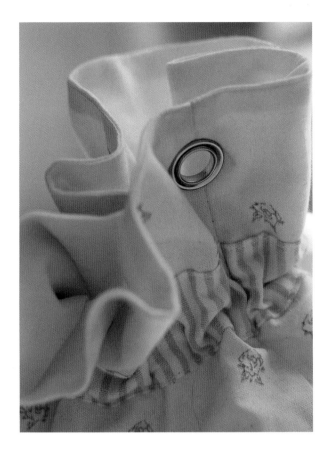

This is what you do:

Cut a piece of material and a piece of lining material measuring 32 x 56cm (12½ x 22½in). Cut a 56 x 3cm (22½ x ⅛in) strip of material for the drawstring channel. Add seam allowances to all of these parts. Iron flat the seam allowance on each side of the drawstring channel. Cut a piece of material measuring about 2.5 x 6cm (1 x 21½in) and place it centrally on the wrong side of the drawstring channel to act as reinforcement at the locations of the holes.

Punch in the small drawstring holes through both layers of material about 2cm (¾in) apart. Cut two pieces of cord about 40cm (15½in) long. Attach the drawstring channel using pins 5cm (2in) from one of the long edges of the material. Place the cords on the channel and thread them through the holes. Sew the drawstring channel around the cord with stitches to fix the ends as in Figure A. Cut out a piece of cotton padding, 56 x 20cm (22½ x 8in), and add a seam allowance. Place the padding along the edge of the lower long edge of the material. Sew it in place with a seam at the top, where the padding ends, and also at the bottom using zigzag stitching, as shown in Figure B.

Cut circles in the material, lining and padding of about 18.5cm (7¼in) in diameter, adding seam allowances. Sew the padding circle to the wrong side of the material circle

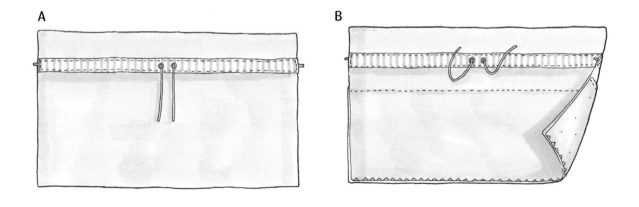

A

B

using zigzag stitching around the edge, as can be seen in Figure C.

Sew the material and lining together along the top edge. Sew the circle of material to form a base on the material of the bag and the circle of lining material in the lining part. Finally, sew along the open edge through the material and lining material, leaving a reversing opening in the lining part. See Figure D. Turn the pompadour inside out through the opening and push the lining part down into the material part.

Iron the pompadour and punch in the large drawstring hole at the top of the back for hanging. Embroider a simple flower as described on page 8 or sew an angel motif as described under 'Wrong Side Appliqués' on page 9.

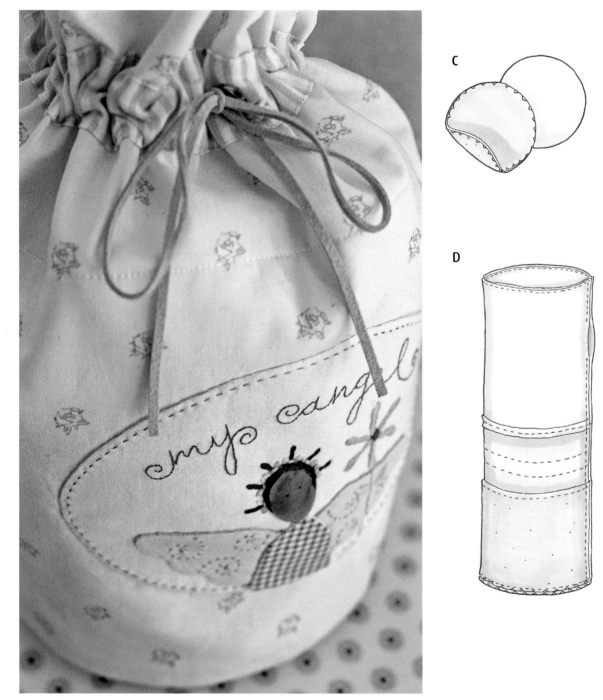

C

D

Make-up Bag

The pattern is on page 138.

You need:

Material
Lining material
Cotton padding filler
Zip fastener, approximately 20cm (8in) long
Embroidery yarn and material for decoration if desired

This is what you do:

Cut two pieces of material, two pieces of padding and two pieces of lining material and add a seam allowance. Attach the padding pieces to the wrong side of the pieces of material by zigzag stitching around the edge, as in Figure A. If desired, decorate one of the pieces of material with appliqués, as described on page 9, or with embroidery, as described on page 8. When locating the motif, remember that the lowest part of the material forms the bottom of the make-up bag.

Place the right side of the zip fastener against the right side of the material along the curved edge and place the liner piece on top with its right side against the material and zip fastener. Sew along the curved edge as shown in Figure B. Fold the material and lining back and attach the other material and lining pieces in the same way to the other side of the zip fastener.

A

B

Open the zip fastener and place the two material pieces and the two lining pieces right side to right side. Sew up the sides and bottom, but leave the corners open. Leave a reversing opening in the lining, as shown in Figure C. Fold the open corners so that the seams are parallel to each other and a base is formed in the material and lining pieces. Sew across the corners, as shown in Figure D.

Cut off the corners and surplus seam allowance and turn the bag inside out. Push the lining down into the bag. If you wish, quilt a seam through all the layers along each side of the zip fastener to keep the lining in place inside the material. See Figure E.

C

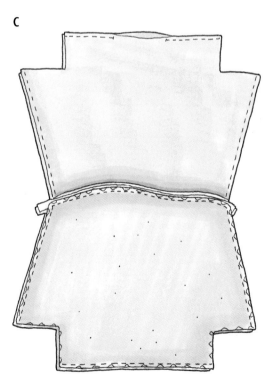

D

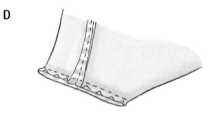

E

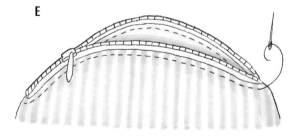

Angel
rose
water

keeps your
skin young
and
beautiful

'Rose Water' Tapestry

The pattern is on page 140.

You probably wonder what you can use to keep your skin looking young and beautiful. Well, according to this tapestry it's Angel Rose Water – which is probably frightfully expensive!

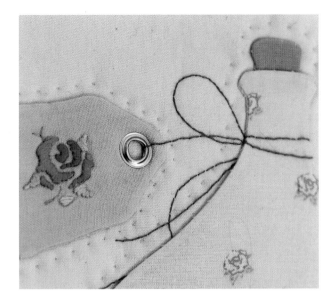

You need:

Materials for the backing and scallop borders
Material for the reverse side
Materials for appliqués
Cotton padding filler
Embroidery yarn
One 6cm (2¼in) drawstring hole for the patch
Two rings for hanging, if desired

This is what you do:

This tapestry resembles the one on page 38, so although the motif is different, the procedure is much the same. Sew the tapestry with scallop edges in the same way as for the tapestry with the cake motif on page 38. Position the words so that the dotted bracket marked on the pattern is along the edge of the backing material. Stitch the wording as described on page 8.

Sew the appliqués on the wrong side, as described on page 9 (bottle, cork, label, tag, two angel's wings, angel's head and angel body). Punch a small drawstring hole through the tag for effect. Position the appliqués on the backing material and tack in place. Embroider and stitch tape for the tag, roses and decorative seam around the tag and on the wings, and embroider hair as described on page 8. Sew up the reversing opening. Quilt around the bottle, the tag, the rose embroidered on the backing material and around the entire edge of the tapestry as described on page 9.

A

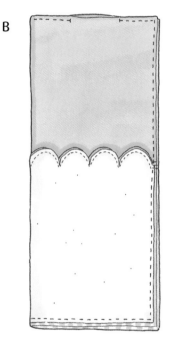

Small Wall Pouches
The pattern for scallop borders is on page 141.

B

You need:

Material
Lining material
Thin vliselin
One 11mm (½in) drawstring hole

This is what you do:

Cut a piece of material, a piece of lining material and a piece of thin vliselin measuring 29 x 19cm (11½ x 7¼in), adding a seam allowance. Iron the vliselin on to the wrong side of the material. If you want, you can embroider a small motif in the centre as described on page 8. Place the lining material and the material together right side to right side. Trace the scallop border along one of the long sides and sew as shown in Figure A. Cut out the scallop border as described on page 10. Fold the lining and material away from each other in opposite directions, so the material is against material and lining against lining. Sew around the edges and leave a reversing opening in the lining, as in Figure B. Fold out the corners in opposite directions and sew across them 2.5cm (1in) from the tip, forming a base in both the material and the lining. See Figure C.

Cut off the corners outside these seams and turn the bag inside out. Push the lining down into the bag and iron it. Punch a small drawstring hole through the back to hang it.

C

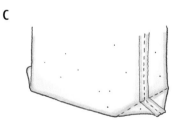

Dressing Gown Angels

Here you see a couple of dressing gown angels, still slightly sleepy and waiting impatiently for the residents of the house to finish their morning routine so that they can have the bathroom to themselves.

Sew the angel's pantaloons (which pass for pyjama bottoms here), slippers and wings as described on pages 59–62.
The dressing gown is sewn in the same way as the jacket on pages 73–74, but using the whole length of the pattern. The small flowers are embroidered as described on page 8.

The angel's towel is made of a piece of material measuring about 15 x 10cm (5½ x 4in). This is folded over double and the edges are then folded in and glued with a glue gun to prevent them from fraying.

Large hearts sewn with woollen felt are decorated with patches, buttons and wording from the 'My House' tapestry described on page 55.

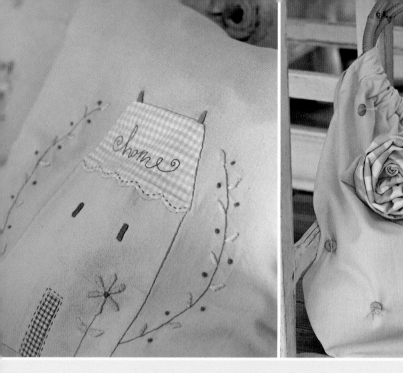

The Bedroom

A bedroom fit for a princess – well, a princess in spirit anyway! The soft blankets are made by simply sewing material and woollen felt together, and need no further description, while all the other items can be found either in this chapter or one of the others. The teddy bear is the same as the one on page 118, but enlarged to 140 per cent.

Hot Water Bottle Cover

The pattern is on page 142

You need:

Woollen felt and material or material and high-volume vliselin for the cover
Material and embroidery yarn for the decorative label
Buttons

This is what you do:

Here I have sewn one hot water bottle cover using woollen felt and another one with fabric. The procedure for each is slightly different.

To start, cut the pattern into two and place the two parts together so that points A and B lie adjacent to each other. The upper and lower buttoned edges overlap each other in the pattern as they will when the two parts are buttoned together. Notice where each part ends.

If the pattern doesn't fit your own hot water bottle, you can use your bottle as a pattern.

Fabric Cover

Cut some material large enough for the whole hot water bottle, adding a seam allowance, and add 2cm (¾in) at the top which can be folded over. Cut an equally large piece of high-volume vliselin, but this should be cut exactly like the pattern at the top. Iron the high-volume vliselin to the wrong side of the material, as in Figure A.

Now cut the top and bottom parts of the front, adding 3cm (1in) of material at the opening on both parts, while the vliselin parts should be cut according to the pattern at the opening. The top should correspond to the top of the whole part, as shown in Figure B.

Fold the large seam allowances in at the buttoned edge at the top and bottom and sew it so that the width of the buttoned edge is as in the pattern. Don't forget that the buttoned edges overlap in the pattern and that they should also be the same width at the top and bottom. Sew three buttonholes on the edge of the upper part and then three buttons on the straight edge of the lower part, as shown in Figure C. Button the parts together. Place the completed front part right side to right side on the back part and sew the two together. Fold down the extra seam allowance around the opening at the top and sew it as in Figure D. Cut off surplus seam allowance and turn the cover inside out.

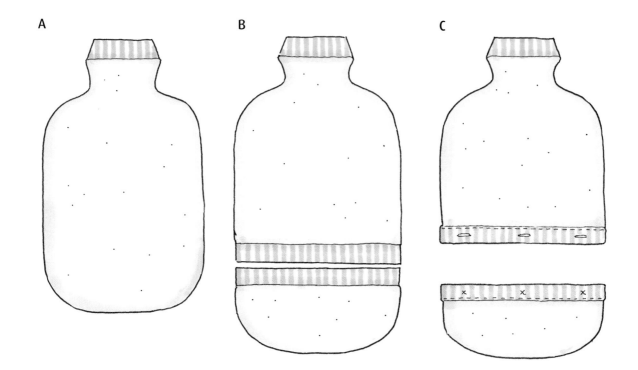

A   B   C

Woollen Felt Cover

No vliselin is used in the felt hot water bottle cover, instead, material is sewn on to make a stable edge for buttoning. Cut out the felt parts as in the pattern but without the buttoned edge. There should normally be a seam allowance around the parts and an extra seam allowance at the opening at the top. Cut two strips of material about 6cm (2½in) wide and as long as the width of the cover and fold them double. Sew these edge pieces to the felt pieces so that they are about 2.5cm (1in) wide, as shown in Figure E. Fold out the edges, sew the buttons and buttonholes and continue as described for the fabric hot water bottle cover.

Decoration

Sew the sign on the wrong side as described on page 9. Stitch the words 'Warm and cosy' and embroider a small flower as described on page 8. Tack the sign to the hot water bottle cover using invisible stitching.

D

E

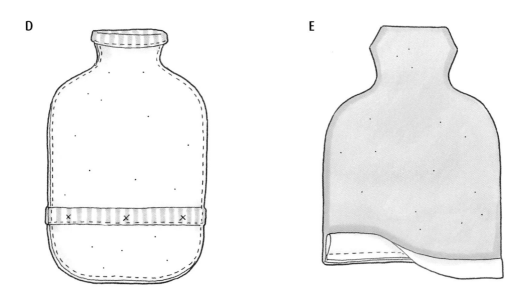

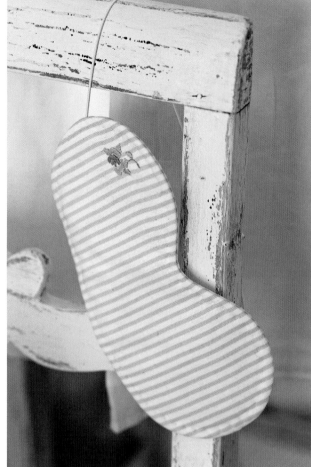

Sleeping Masks
The pattern is on page 141

You need:

Material
Cotton padding
Thin elastic
Embroidery yarn for decoration if desired

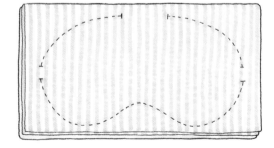

This is what you do:

Fold a piece of material large enough to cover the pattern double and place on top of a piece of padding large enough to cover the pattern once. Trace the mask and sew around the edge, as in the figure, left. Leave a small opening for the elastic on each side of the mask as well as a reversing opening, as shown on the pattern. Hold the end of a piece of elastic at your left temple, stretch it around the back of your head to the right temple, and cut this length. Don't make it too tight. Place the elastic between the material layers with each end emerging from the small holes at the sides. Sew back and forth to attach the elastic. Cut out the mask and turn it inside out. If you like, you can embroider a small rose or similar decoration as described on page 8, and quilt around the edge as described on page 9.

Leaf Wall Pouches

You need:

Material
High-volume vliselin
Drawstring holes, about 11mm (½in) diameter
or coat hanger and press studs

This is what you do:

There are two versions of the leaf wall pouches, one to hang right on the wall using three draw-string holes, while the other is buttoned around a coat hanger.

Hung using holes

Cut two pieces of material and a piece of high-volume vliselin measuring 74 x 26.5cm (29 x 10½in) and add seam allowances. Iron the high-volume vliselin to the wrong side of one piece of the material.

Cut four pieces of material and two pieces of high-volume vliselin measuring each 21 x 26.5cm (8¼ x 10½in) for the pouches and add seam allowances. Iron the high-volume vliselin to the wrong side of two of the pieces of material. Now we'll call the pieces of material without vliselin 'lining'.

Place the material and lining for the pouches together right side to right side. Trace, sew and turn the pouch and scallop border inside out, as described on page 10. Sew a zigzag seam around the edge to keep the layers together, as shown in Figure A.

Sew the two pouches in place, one 5cm (2in) from the lower edge and the other 37cm (14½in) from the lower edge. The pouches should be pointing downwards when sewn on, as in Figure B. Fold the pouches upwards and sew them in place with zigzag stitching, as shown in Figure C.

Place the lining piece right side to right side on the pouch piece and sew around, leaving a reversing opening. Cut off any surplus seam allowance and turn the bag inside out. Sew a seam 5cm (2in) below the upper edge and punch in three drawstring holes, as shown in Figure D.

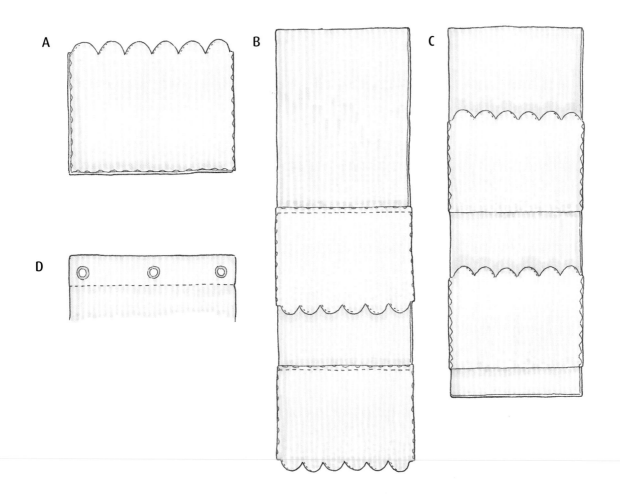

Hung using coat hanger

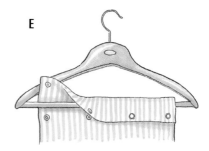

If you want to hang the leaf wall pouch using a coat hanger it is sewn in the same way, but with an additional 5cm (2in) at the top, which is folded around the coat hanger. The dimensions of the backing piece are therefore 79 x 26.5cm (31 x 10½in).

Attach four press-stud top pieces about 1cm (½in) from the top, and four bottom pieces about 9cm (3½in) from the top. Notice which way the parts of the press-studs must face so that they will fasten together. Button the leaf wall pouch around the cross-piece of the coat hanger, as shown in Figure E.

Bear

This bear is the same as you can see on page 119, but it is 140 per cent larger.

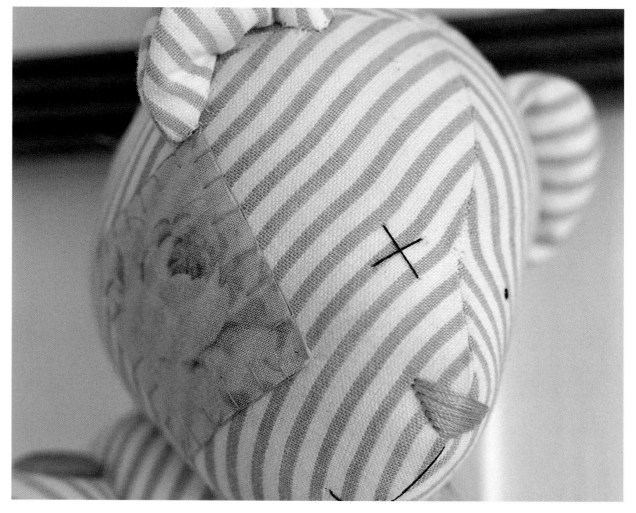

The Children's Room

The children's room contains all the figures in this book. A flying horse with angel's wings is hanging beneath the bed canopy. The pussy cat is sleeping in the doll's bed and the dog is making sure there are no monsters under the bed. The teddy bears are holding a tea party and discussing the events of the day. Large strawberries function both as cushions and toys.

NB: Make sure to consider the age of your children when deciding which toys are safe to put in their bedrooms.

A simple wall board can be made out of a stretcher frame covered with material. Use a glue gun to attach tapes in a criss-cross pattern, sewing on a button or pom-pom at each intersection, as shown.

Teddy Bears

The pattern is on page 143.

You need:

Material for the body
Material and vlisofix for patches
Woollen felt for the sweater
Material for the shorts
Embroidery yarn
Four buttons
Stuffing

NB: Small objects like buttons can be dangerous for young children, so consider whether this toy is suitable for the age of your child.

This is what you do:

The teddy bears in the children's room are sewn to the same size as the pattern, while the striped bear found in the bedroom is enlarged to 140 per cent.

Sew the teddy bear in the same way as the cat on page 32, except that you should fix the arms and legs firmly to the body using buttons and embroidery yarn, as shown in Figure A. This way the arms and legs will be movable and the teddy bear will be more fun to play with.

Sew small lines on the paws for claws, as shown in Figure B. Sew the felt sweater in the same way as the sweater for the angel on page 60.

A

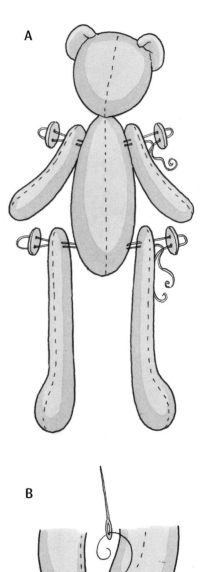

B

Cut out the parts for the teddy bear's shorts, adding a good seam allowance at the top and bottom. Place the parts right side to right side and sew them together as shown in Figure C. Fold the shorts the opposite way and sew the legs up, as in Figure D. Iron the seam allowance in place using vlisofix and turn the shorts inside out.

Attach the shorts to the teddy bear with a few stitches around the waist and put on the sweater. Fold the neck of the sweater in the same way as for the angel on page 60.

Finally, patches in various sizes are ironed on using vlisofix and sewn around with buttonhole stitching. Make a face for the teddy bear as described on page 11, but replace one eye with a small, stitched cross. Sew a stitch down from the nose and one across to form a mouth, as in Figure E.

C

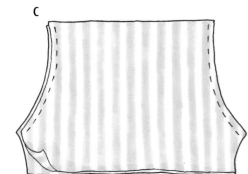

D

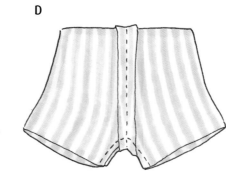

E

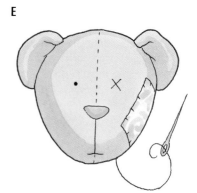

Strawberry Cushions

The pattern is on page 144.

When I was younger, I wished that I could be tiny, so that I could sleep in a matchbox and be full up after eating a wild strawberry. That's why it's so much fun to make larger-than-life things; you can pretend that you are tiny.

Sew the strawberries in the same way as the small ones on page 36. The same materials are also used.

   Notice that the pattern has been cut to fit to the page; place the two parts together so that the points A and B lie adjacent to each other. The pattern also has a fold-line on it and should be twice as large.

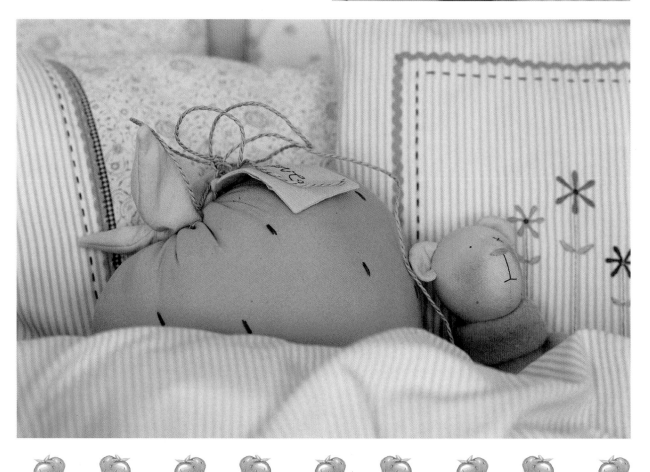

Thank you

The photos for the book were taken at the Kunstforeningen Verdens Ende, an art club in Budalsgården that used to be a rectory, dating from the 1820s, on the island of Tjøme. The house is frequently used for exhibitions and events all year round and is well worth a visit.

The photographer, Grethe Syvertsen Arnstad, and the stylist, Ingrid Skonfar, brought the beautiful sunshine and worked wonders with an enthusiasm and imagination that made me speechless with admiration. Accompanied by Jørn, who lives alone in the house, with his wonderfully helpful nature, we had an enormously enjoyable time on those sunny days.

I am really fortunate to have a fantastic interior decorating shop, called 'Tinnies Hus' in the neighbouring town. Here they happily lent us all the furniture and props we could desire. Tinnies Hus is in Tollbodgaten 19 in Tønsberg.

The furnishings for the conservatory and the lovely flowers came from a beautiful little florist's shop called 'Tornerose' in Storgaten 41, Tønsberg.

I personally want to thank these shops specially for their contributions, which exceeded all our expectations and are still a source of inspiration.

A big thank you also to:
'Dinas Hus' and 'Rørleggerbutikken' on Tjøme, 'Frisk Bris' on Hvasser, 'Gallery Gudem' in Tønsberg, 'Noa Noa' in Tønsberg, Tove, Jørn, Åge and Gerd, Torje, and of course Totto. I would also like to thank all my good friends who are always willing to help, particularly Eirin.

Addresses

Coast and Country Crafts & Quilts
Tel: 01872 863894
coastandcountrycrafts@
yahoo.co.uk

Coats and Clark USA
PO Box 12229
Greenville SC29612-0229
Tel: 0800 648 1479
www.coatsandclark.com

Fred Aldous Ltd.
37 Lever Street
Manchester
Tel 08707 517301
www.fredaldous.co.uk

Panduro Hobby
Westway House
Transport Avenue
Brentford
Tel: 020 8566 1680
www.panduro.co.uk

Quiltzauberei.de
Marschallstr. 9
46539 Dinslaken
Germany
Tel: +49 2064 827980
www.quiltzauberei.de

The Fat Quarters
5 Choprell Road
Blackhall Mill
Newcastle
Tel: 01207 565728
www.thefatquarters.co.uk

The Sewing Bee
52 Hillfoot Street
Dunoon
Argyll
Tel: 01369 706879
www.thesewingbee.co.uk

Threads and Patches
48 Aylesbury Street
Fenny Stratford, Bletchley
Tel: 01908 649687
www.threadsandpatches.co.uk

Patterns

A page reference for the pattern can be found in the instructions for each project. Openings are marked by dotted lines.

ES stands for 'extra seam allowance' and is used in places where a particularly wide seam is thought necessary. Always sew out seam allowances which end at an opening. Woollen felt doesn't fray, so seam allowances aren't necessary at openings and along edges which are to be sewn to something else. These are marked on the pattern with dotted lines, which should be cut along.

EMBROIDERY MOTIF

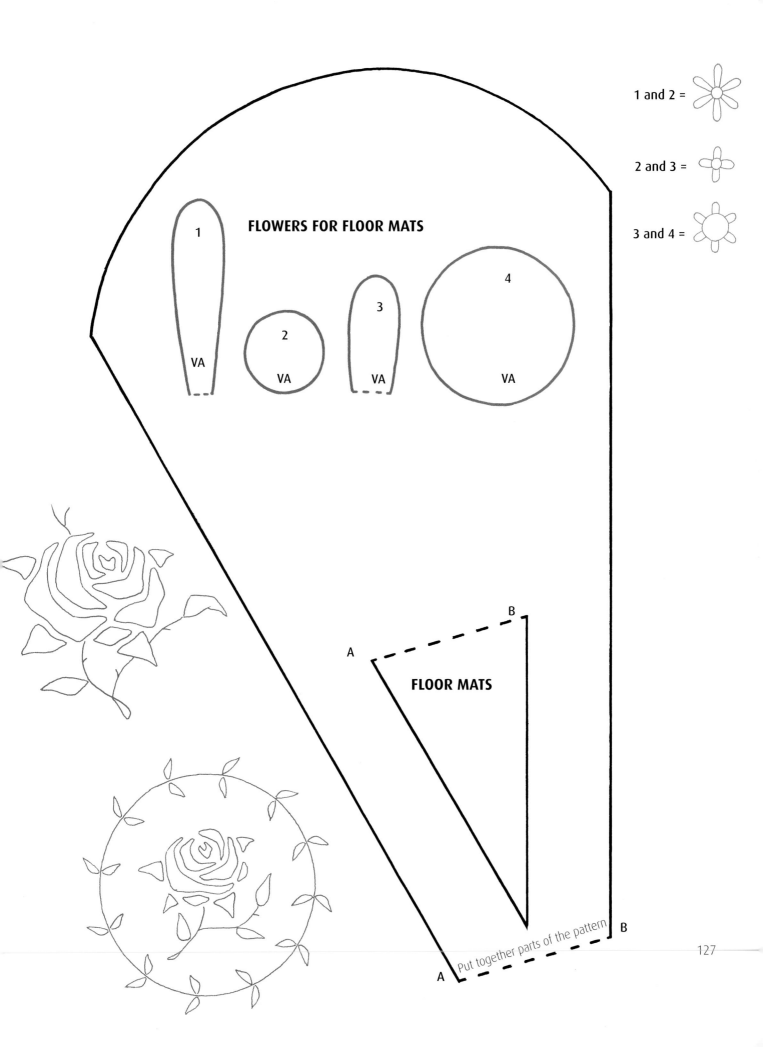

1 and 2 =

2 and 3 =

3 and 4 =

FLOWERS FOR FLOOR MATS

1

VA

2

VA

3

VA

4

VA

B

A

FLOOR MATS

B

Put together parts of the pattern

A

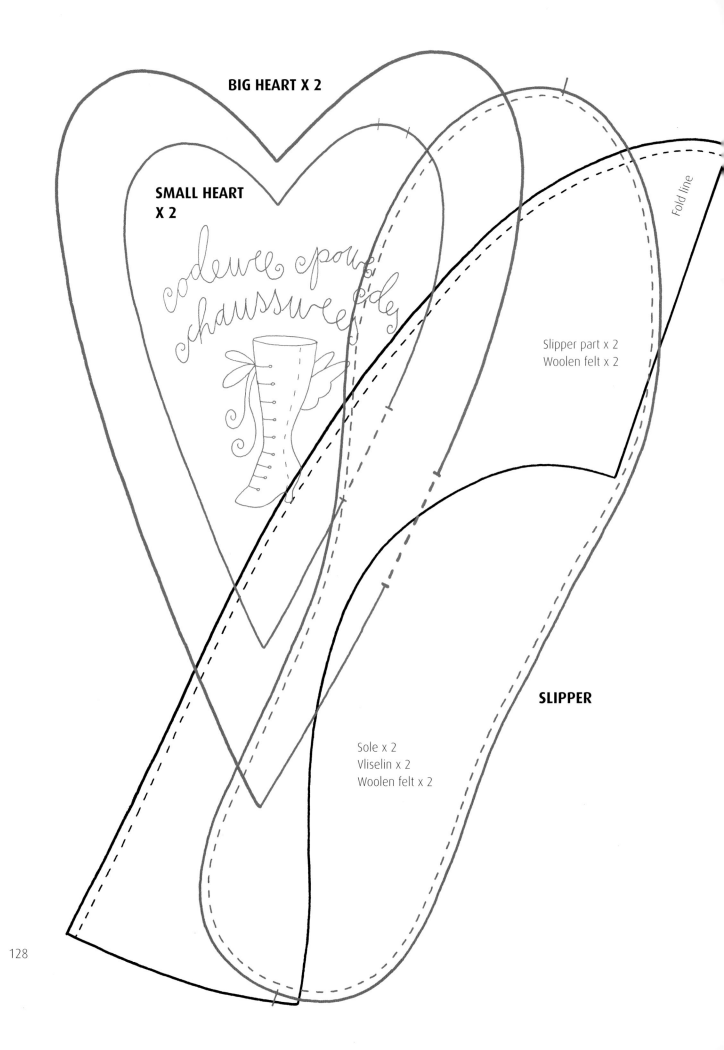

BIG HEART X 2

SMALL HEART X 2

Slipper part x 2
Woolen felt x 2

SLIPPER

Sole x 2
Vliselin x 2
Woolen felt x 2

Fold line

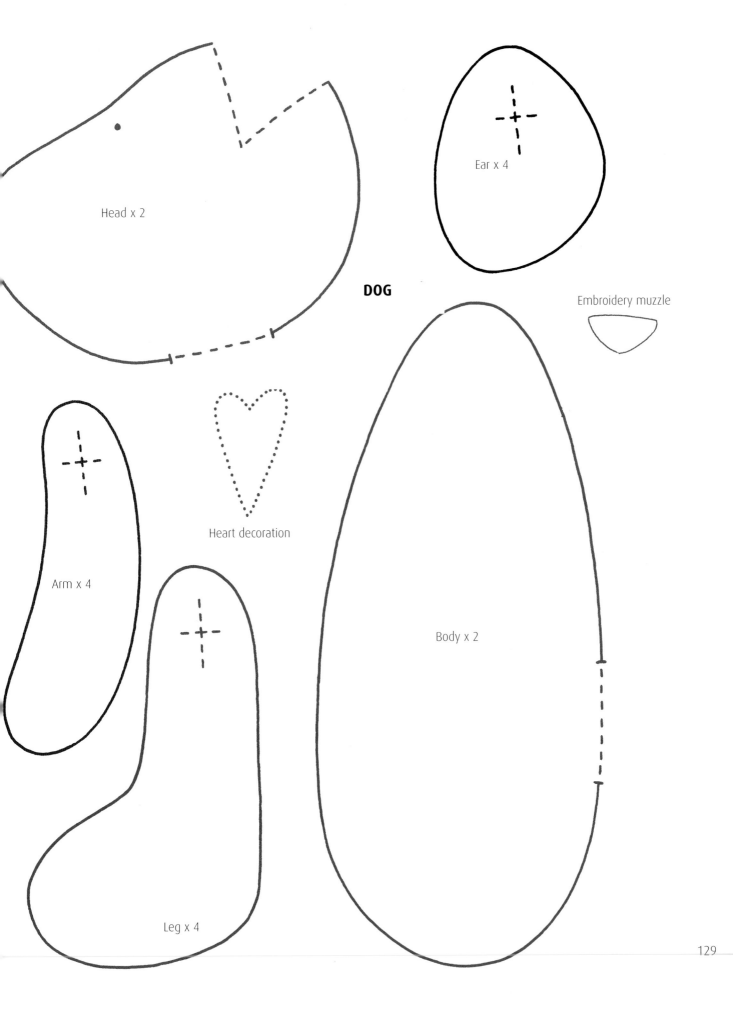

Head x 2

Ear x 4

DOG

Embroidery muzzle

Heart decoration

Arm x 4

Body x 2

Leg x 4

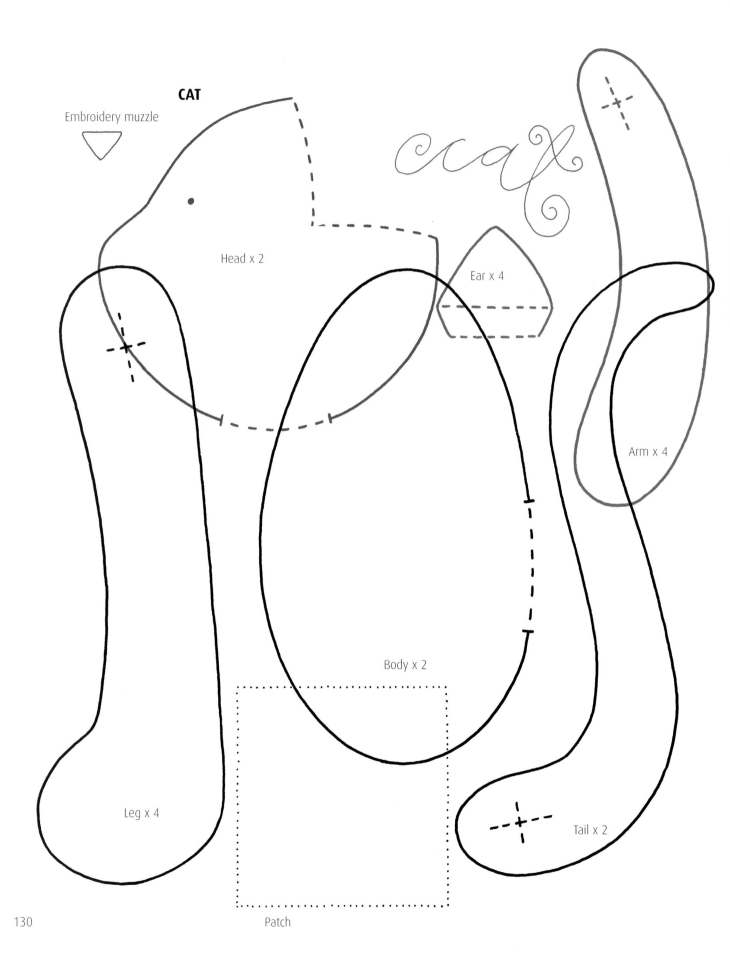

CAT

Embroidery muzzle

Head x 2

Ear x 4

Arm x 4

Body x 2

Leg x 4

Tail x 2

Patch

130

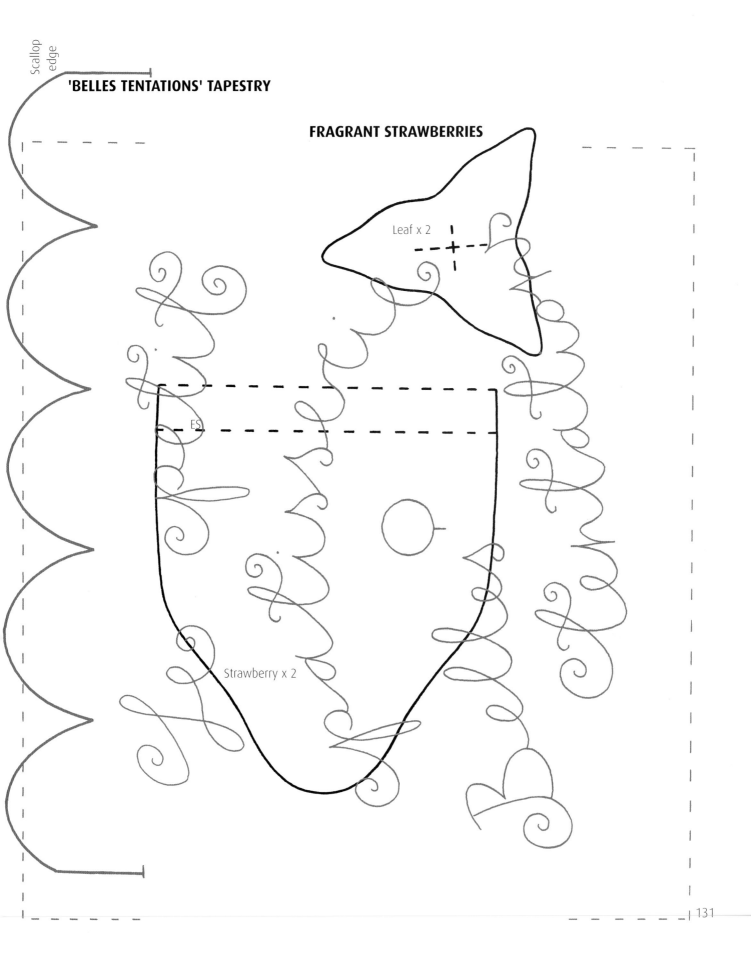

'BELLES TENTATIONS' TAPESTRY

FRAGRANT STRAWBERRIES

Leaf x 2

ES

Strawberry x 2

CAKE DISH
(for 'Belle Tentation')

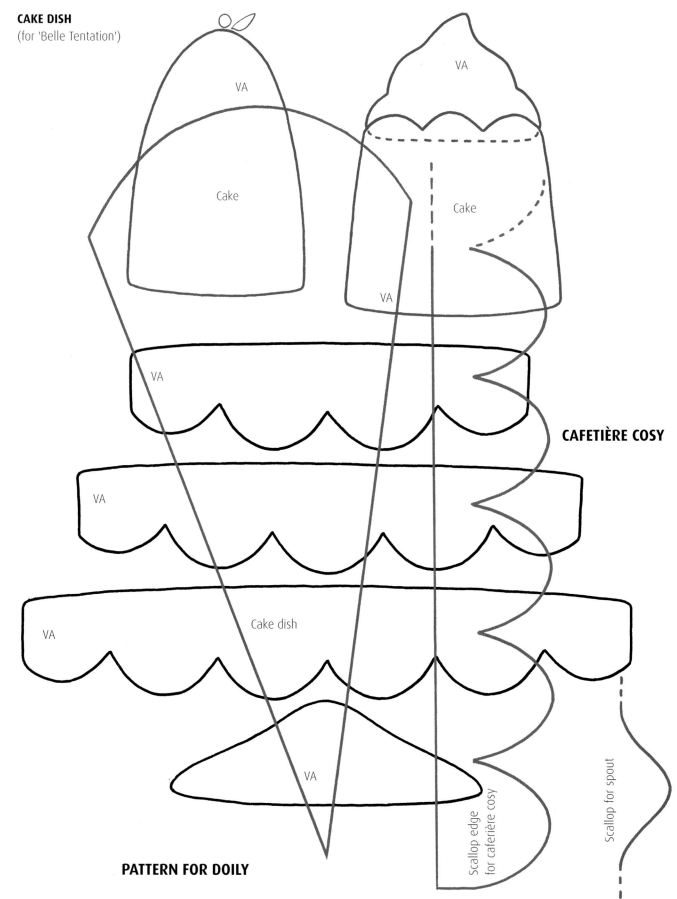

VA

VA

Cake

Cake

VA

VA

CAFETIÈRE COSY

VA

VA

VA

Cake dish

VA

Scallop edge
for caferière cosy

Scallop for spout

PATTERN FOR DOILY

'MY HOUSE' TAPESTRY

Embroidered chimneys

VA

VA

VA

VA

VA

Embroidered window

Fold line for small house

Fold line for medium house

Fold line for small house

Door

VA

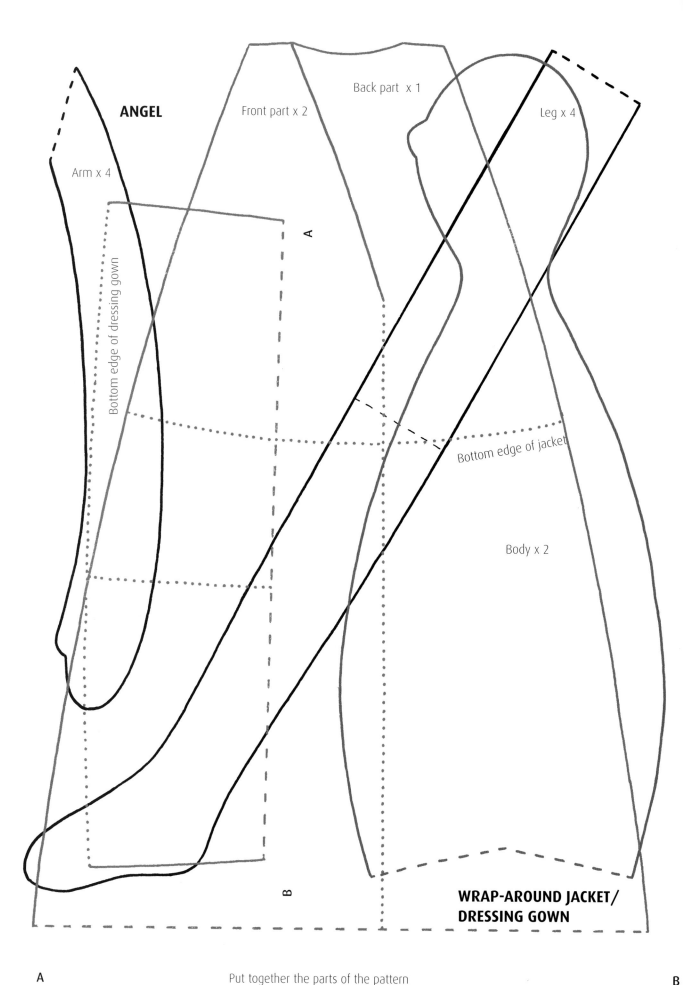

ANGEL

Arm x 4

Front part x 2

Back part x 1

Leg x 4

A

Bottom edge of dressing gown

Bottom edge of jacket

Body x 2

B

WRAP-AROUND JACKET/
DRESSING GOWN

A

Put together the parts of the pattern

B

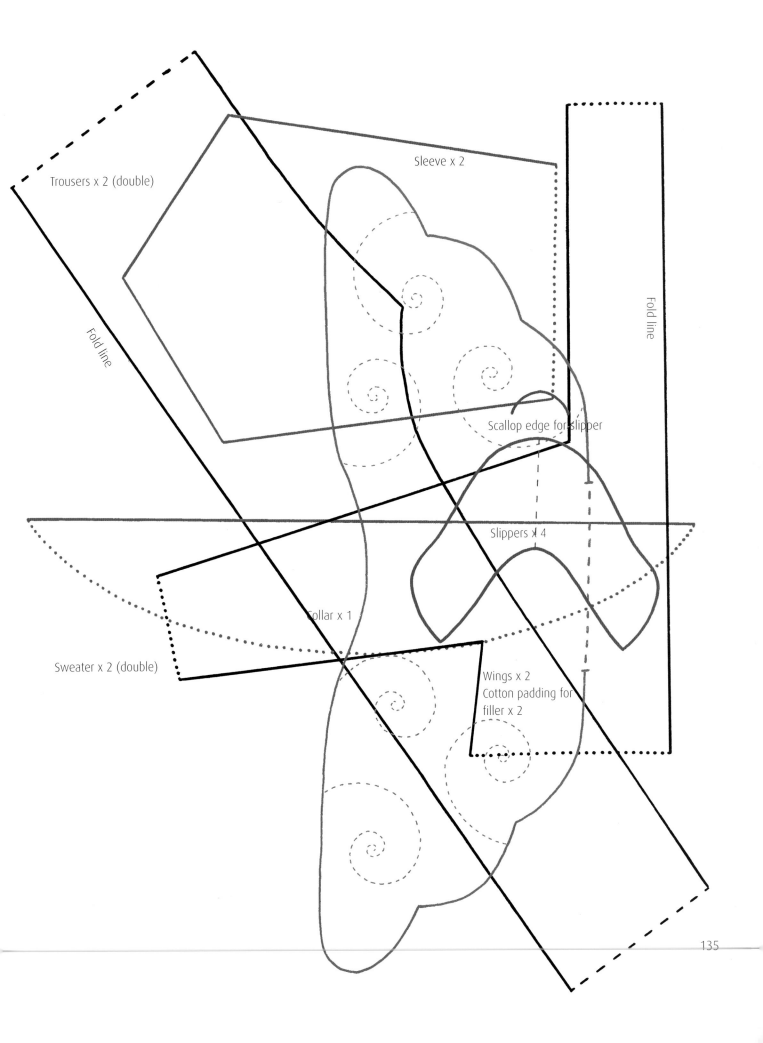

Trousers x 2 (double)

Sleeve x 2

Fold line

Fold line

Scallop edge for slipper

Slippers x 4

Collar x 1

Sweater x 2 (double)

Wings x 2
Cotton padding for
filler x 2

135

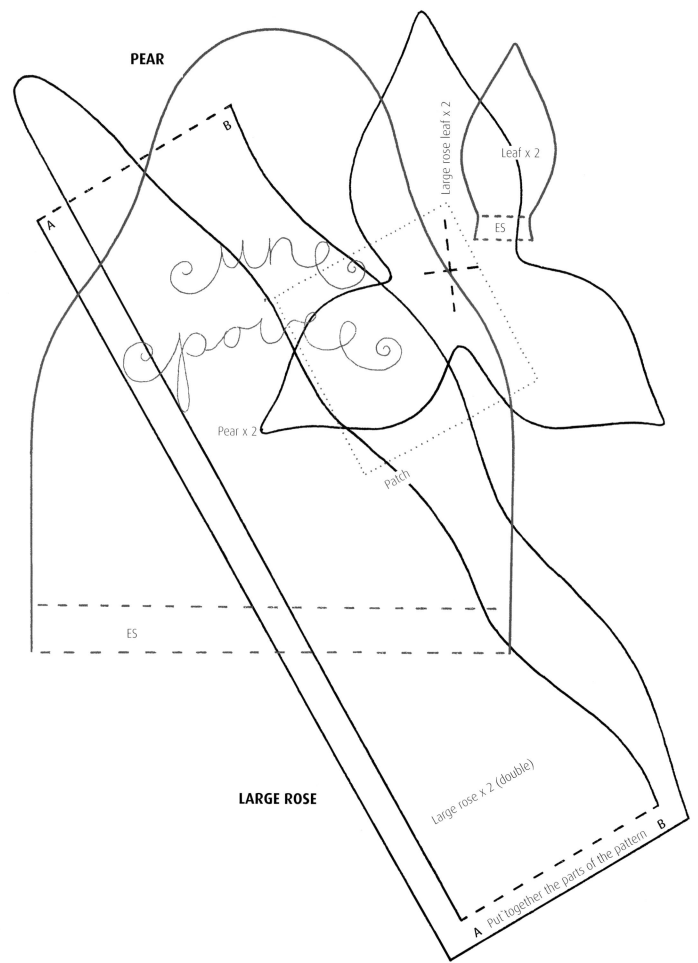

PEAR

B

A

Large rose leaf x 2

Leaf x 2

ES

Pear x 2

Patch

ES

LARGE ROSE

Large rose x 2 (double)

A   Put together the parts of the pattern   B

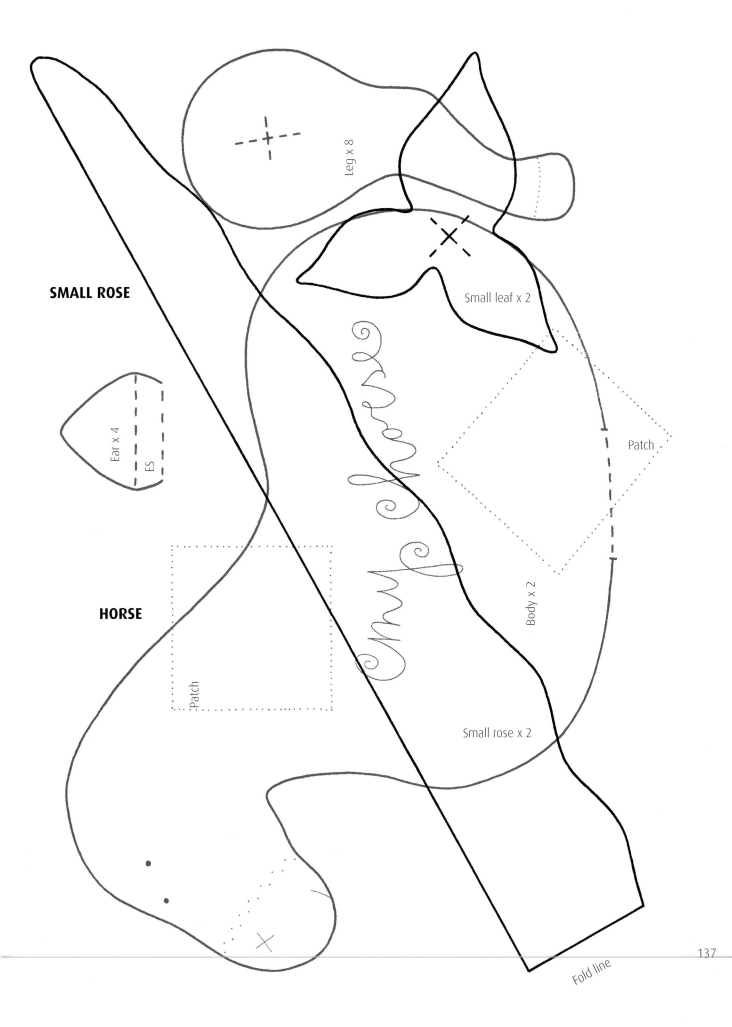

SMALL ROSE

Leg x 8

Small leaf x 2

Ear x 4

ES

HORSE

Patch

Body x 2

Patch

Small rose x 2

Fold line

137

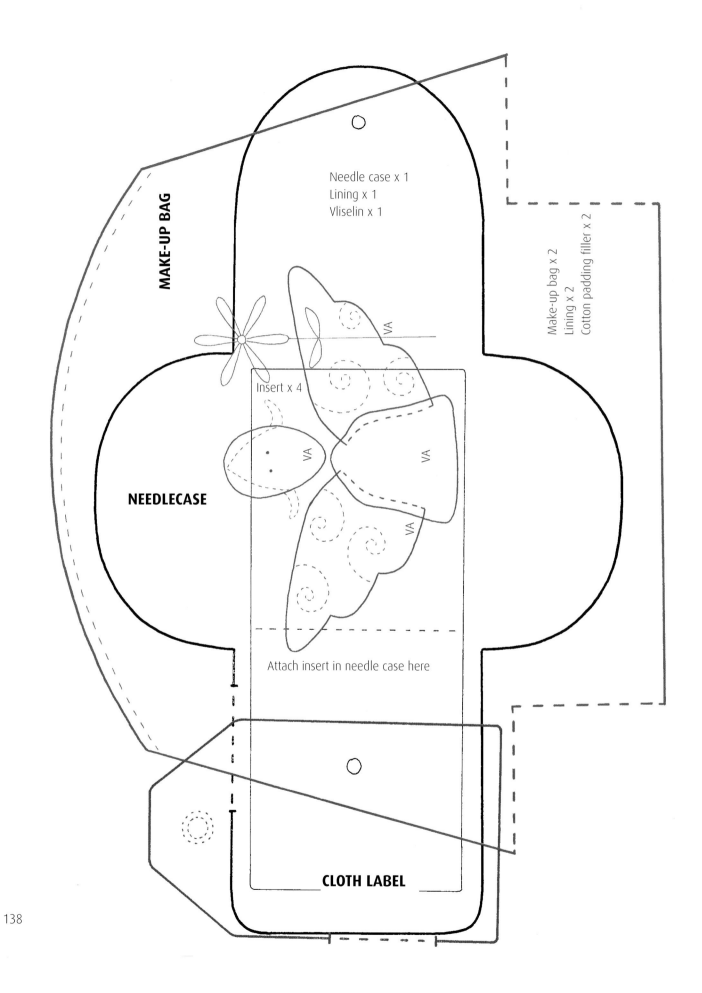

MAKE-UP BAG

Needle case x 1
Lining x 1
Vliselin x 1

Make-up bag x 2
Lining x 2
Cotton padding filler x 2

Insert x 4

VA

VA

VA

VA

NEEDLECASE

Attach insert in needle case here

CLOTH LABEL

MOTIF FOR PIN CUSHION

MOTIF FOR BUTTON BAG

MOTIF FOR POMPADOUR

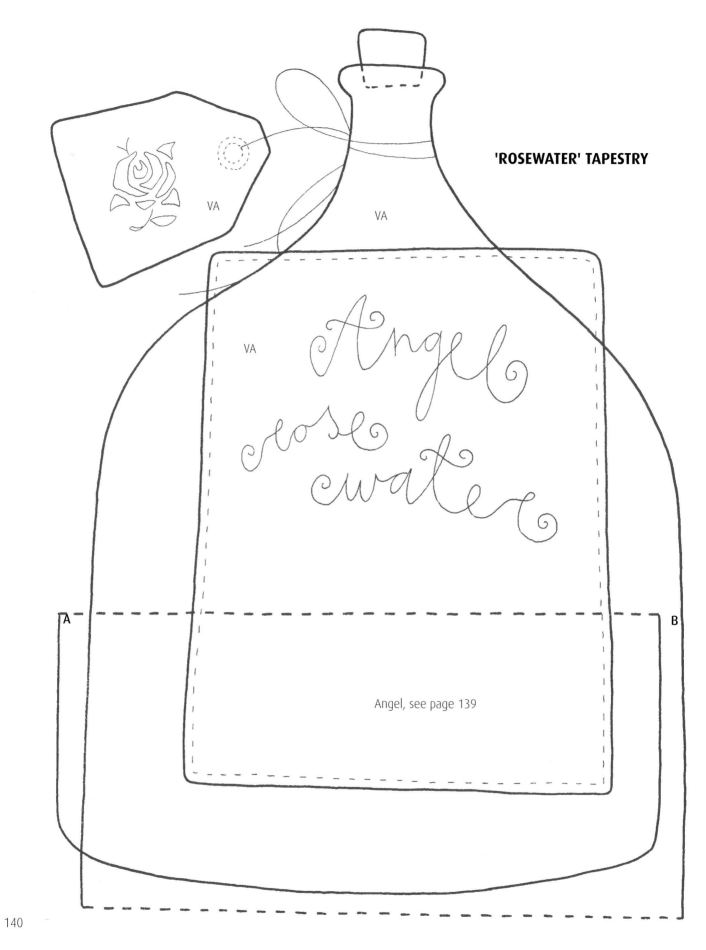

'ROSEWATER' TAPESTRY

VA

VA

VA

Angel rose water

Angel, see page 139

A

B

A

Put together the parts of the pattern

B

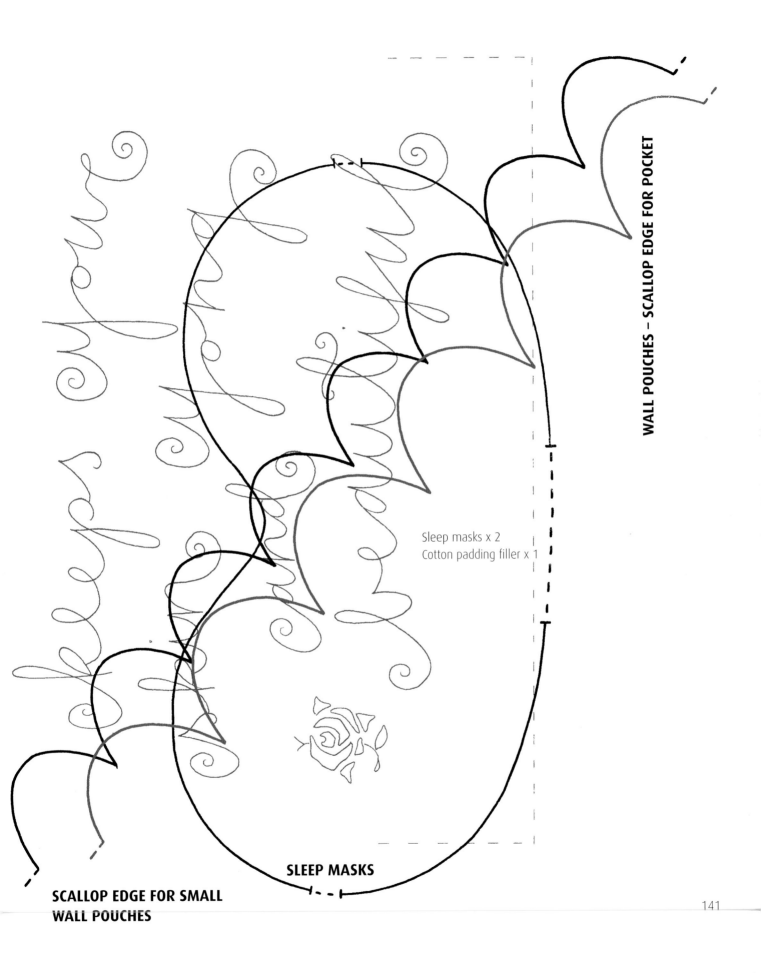

WALL POUCHES – SCALLOP EDGE FOR POCKET

Sleep masks x 2
Cotton padding filler x 1

SLEEP MASKS

**SCALLOP EDGE FOR SMALL
WALL POUCHES**

HOT WATER BOTTLE COVER

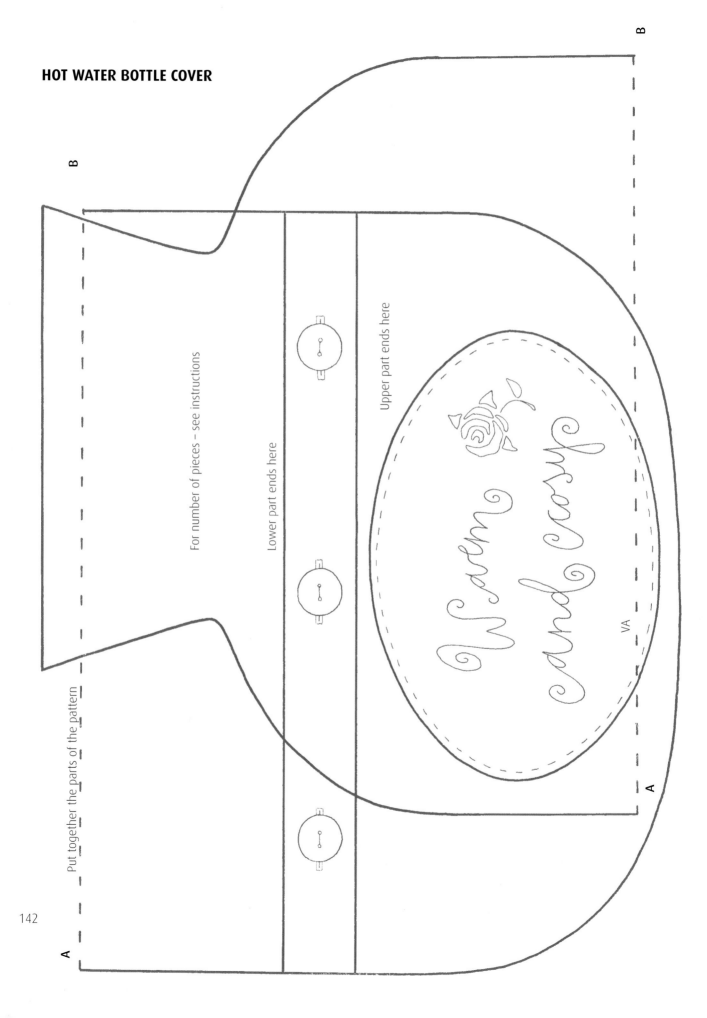

Put together the parts of the pattern

For number of pieces – see instructions

Lower part ends here

Upper part ends here

Warm and cosy

VA

142

TEDDYBEAR

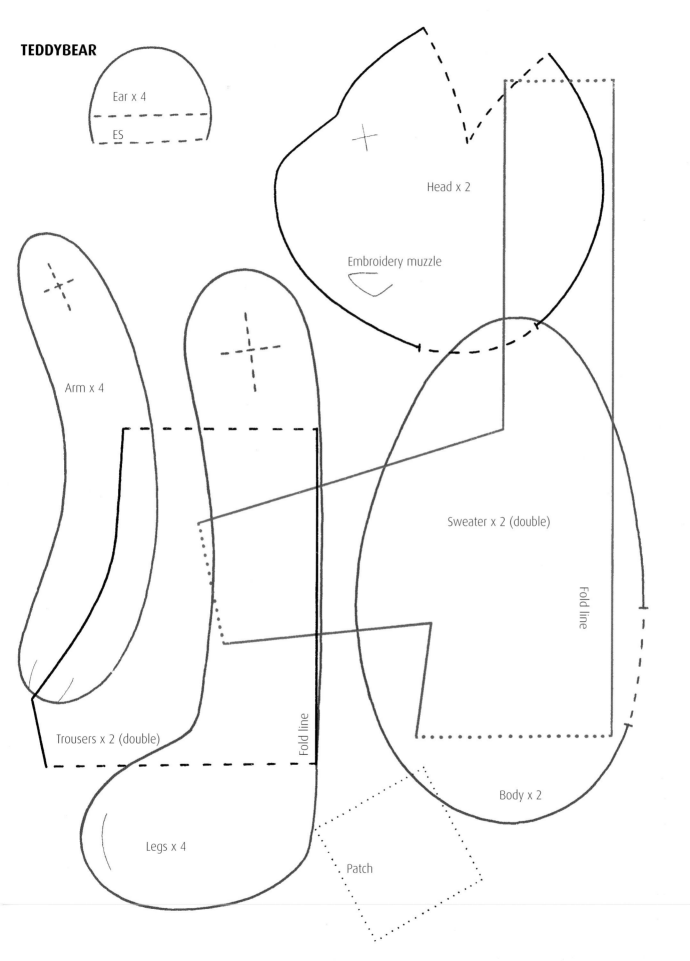

Ear x 4

ES

Head x 2

Embroidery muzzle

Arm x 4

Sweater x 2 (double)

Fold line

Trousers x 2 (double)

Fold line

Fold line

Body x 2

Legs x 4

Patch

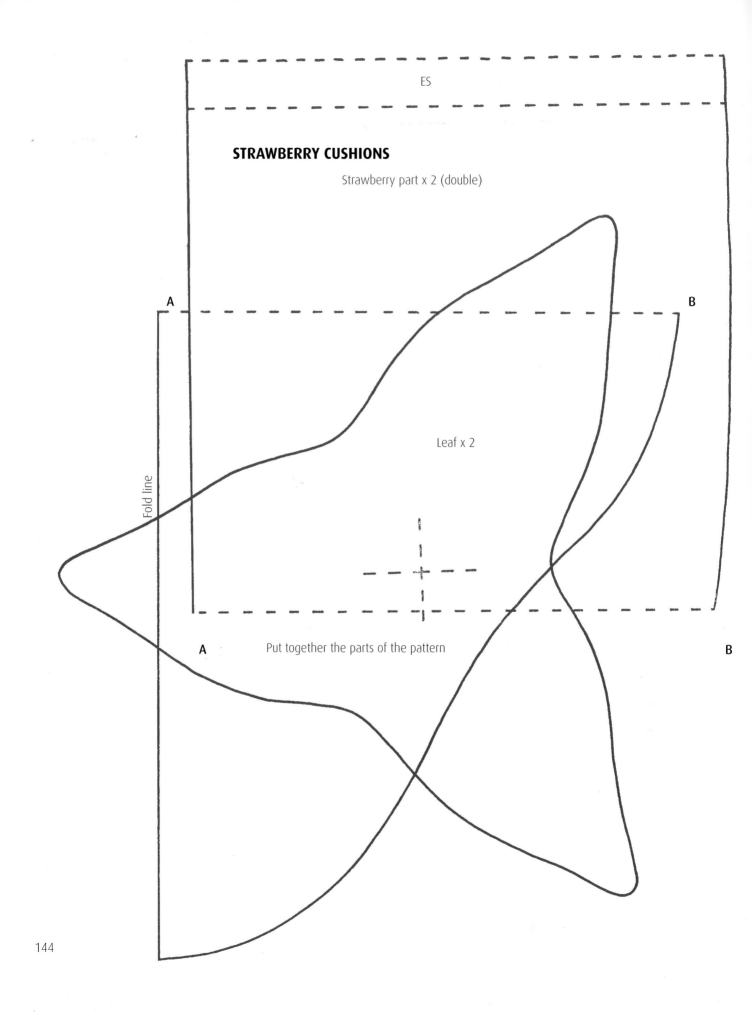

ES

STRAWBERRY CUSHIONS

Strawberry part x 2 (double)

A

B

Leaf x 2

Fold line

A

Put together the parts of the pattern

B